Lost Restaurants
OF
LOUISVILLE

Lost Restaurants

OF

LOUISVILLE

STEPHEN HACKER & MICHELLE TURNER

AMERICAN PALATE

Published by American Palate

A Division of The History Press

Charleston, SC

www.historypress.net

First published 2015

Manufactured in the United States

ISBN 978.1.46711.812.5

Library of Congress Control Number: 2015949290

For Buffy, who is very fond of restaurants.

CONTENTS

Acknowledgements   9
Introduction   11

1. Kolb's: Rolled Oysters in a League of Their Own   13
2. Bauer's: From Ponies to "Preppies"   15
3. Cuscaden's: Ice Cream Is "a Food"   19
4. Mazzoni's: Oyster Rush Over, Rolled Oysters Remain   21
5. Vienna: Rescued by Democrats, Ruined by Fire   25
6. Miller's: Nearly One Hundred Years of Home Cooking   28
7. Benedict's: Spending Immortality as a Spread   31
8. Senning's: Successfully Following Streetcars to South Louisville   36
9. Kunz's: Flying "The Dutchman" Around Downtown   38
10. Colonnade: Innovative Service and Unforgettable Pies   44
11. Cunningham's: Fallen Women, Fish Sandwiches and a Flexible
    Approach to the Law   48
12. Little Tavern: White Castle? What White Castle?   51
13. China Inn: "Chop Suey," Cave Hill, Congress and
    the Cabbage Patch   53
14. Canary Cottage: Strange Lands Lead to Shaker Recipes   56
15. Blue Boar: A "Home-Cooked" Meal with a Side of History
    and Heritage   60
16. Stebbins: Seafood, Swank and Swizzle   66
17. Kaelin's: Bootlegger to "Birthplace" of the Cheeseburger   69

CONTENTS

18. Hasenour's: Turning Friendship into a Legend   73
19. Luvisi's: From Italian Novelty to Louisville Institution   80
20. Kupie's: Copyright-Skirting Cuteness Across from the Cathedral   85
21. The Plantation: An Elaborate, Embarrassing Way to Symbolize
    a City   88
22. Leo's Hideaway: A Bet Begins a Louisville Aristocrat   91
23. The Old House: Intriguing History Meets Irascible, Independent
    Woman   94
24. Stewart's Orchid Room: White Gloves, Mayonnaise and Murals   100
25. C-54 Grill: The Restaurant that Got Its Wings   105
26. Hick's, Southwind and Pryors: Leading Louisville into the
    Postwar Suburbs   107
27. Melrose Inn: From Attracting Motorists to Owning the Derby   109
28. Li'l Abner's: Dogpatch Comes "Home"   112
29. Hoe Kow: Bringing Louisville "Something Exotic"   115
30. simmons: Lowering Cases, Losing Customers   123
31. Ferd Grisanti's: Plaster Flamingos Forgone for Four-Star
    Reputation   127
32. Jay's: Fighting Prejudice with Family-Style Food   131
33. The Fig Tree: Fighting a Ghost, Forging the Mettle of "Louisville's
    Alice Waters"   134
34. Sixth Avenue: Setting Standards, Seeding Chefs   138
35. Cafe Metro: Making Bardstown Road "Restaurant Row"   141
36. Afro-German Tea Room: Rescuing a Parish with a Restaurant   146
37. De La Torre's: Studiously Spanish for Over Two Decades   150
38. Timothy's: Louisville's White Chili "Inventors"   152
39. Deitrich's: Freemasonry Fosters Frankfort Avenue's
    Restaurant Row   155
40. La Paloma: Ruffling Regulars, Regaining Loyalty with
    Small Plates   160

Bibliography   163
Index   167
About the Authors   171

ACKNOWLEDGEMENTS

We are grateful to John Nation, Susan Reigler, Richard Des Ruisseaux, Greg Haynes, Bim Deitrich, Nancy Shepherd, Alan Rupp, Greg Haner, Paul Grisanti, Kathy Cary, Susan Seiller, Ray Simmons, Laura Leong, Lee Luvisi, Jenny Ballard, Denis Kitchen and many others who allowed us their time, photographs and memorabilia. We especially appreciate the informative and helpful Keith Runyon, who granted more of his time than we deserve. We would also like to thank the staff of the Filson Society, the University of Louisville archives and the Louisville Free Public Library—all of whom were unfailingly patient, gracious and giving on multiple occasions. And many thanks to Jo Altemeyer for her incomparable transcription skills.

INTRODUCTION

Along with bats, bourbon whiskey and an early May horse race, Louisville has become famous for its restaurants. KFC and Papa John's Pizza are known around the world. Celebrity chefs and stellar cuisine consistently gain national attention. Louisville's restaurants date back almost to the founding of the city, when taverns and hotels sprang up to serve pioneers moving westward after the Revolutionary War. And while Original Recipe®, Hot Browns and Benedictine may all be delicious, they are only appetizers for the interesting, odd and occasionally profane stories of Louisville's legendary restaurants. Arranged roughly in the order of their establishment, these restaurants left Louisville with signature dishes, arresting architecture and outsized personalities. While we couldn't include every amazing story of Louisville's former restaurants, we believe we have provided a broad and rich portrait of many of the restaurants that set the table for today's dining scene. We've also provided recipes to help re-create several dishes from Louisville's lost restaurants. *Bon appétit*!

Chapter 1

KOLB'S

Rolled Oysters in a League of Their Own

The giant Louisville Slugger bat on Main Street is an obvious sign that, in Derby City, the roots of "America's pastime" run deep. Some of those roots were a little dirty, but Al Kolb and his tavern helped clean them up.

By 1857, baseball had become so popular that New York's Knickerbocker Club asked several neighboring teams to assemble and agree upon a standardized set of rules, including forbidding any player from receiving payment. This "National Association" did not last long, and paying players became a common practice. By 1869, the Cincinnati Red Stockings became baseball's first professional club, and within a few years, others joined under the "National Association of Professional Baseball Players." It was a loose organization in every sense of the word, and gambling and bribery soon became widespread. America was beginning to see baseball as seamy, sleazy and unattractive. Several club owners decided to do something about it. A Louisville bar was where they chose to do it.

Tony Montedonico opened a tavern at 323 West Liberty in 1865. At the end of the bar was a small back room where, in 1875, representatives from Louisville, Chicago, Cincinnati and St. Louis agreed to form the National League. Expelling players for "selling malt or spirituous liquors on the league grounds" helped elevate baseball's reputation. And even after Montedonico's tavern passed to Al Kolb, the back room kept its connection to baseball. Kolb said many "old-time baseball greats," such as Pete Browning (the original "Louisville Slugger"), would stop by, with one sports columnist suggesting the little back room "should be

Kolb's, where baseball's National League was formed. *Courtesy of University of Louisville.*

preserved for posterity, were it possible to dismantle and reconstruct it in baseball's hall of fame at Cooperstown."

Until Kolb's closed in 1947, the little downtown tavern also remained connected to another Louisville tradition—the rolled oyster. Kentucky culinary author Marion Flexner wrote that Al Kolb "insisted his mother brought the recipe [for rolled oysters] from New Orleans," competing with the Mazzoni family's more accepted claim that they invented the "fist-sized, croquetted affair" in the 1870s.

Razed as part of urban renewal, the site of the formation of the National League is now part of the Hyatt hotel and parking garage complex. But baseball and the rolled oyster are still parts of the city.

Chapter 2
BAUER'S

From Ponies to "Preppies"

By 1870, things had settled down enough from the Civil War that a smithy could open on the road between Louisville and Brownsboro, a farming community in what is now Oldham County. Originally a dirt track traced by pre–Revolutionary War settlers, the "Louisville & Brownsborough Turnpike Road" had become a for-profit enterprise, with travelers forced to pay a toll so "pikes" barring their way would be "turned" to allow passage. John Bauer set up his shop just about a mile east of the Louisville tollgate—a place to get a horse shod, a wagon repaired and perhaps some supplies. Bauer's wife began serving soups and sandwiches to people waiting for their horses and wagons.

By the 1920s, the automobile was making smithies obsolete and suburban development was spreading around Bauer's. An antique bar brought in around 1890 helped the business, but Mrs. Bauer's food helped more. John Bauer's son, Albert, saw the future, took over and made Bauer's a restaurant. The area surrounding the former turnpike became a wealthy suburban neighborhood, especially after World War II. By then, Albert Bauer had become a successful restaurateur and banker. He died in 1953, leaving sons Arthur and Albert Jr. in charge. As the restaurant continued its popularity, the Bauers began giving up living quarters to increase the area in which they could entertain.

A 1954 *Louisville Times* dining guide described Bauer's as a place "where gracious dining has been enjoyed by discriminating people since 1870," famous for its "delicious Dutch Plate and special Smearkase." The spreadable

Bauer's patio. *Courtesy of John Nation.*

fresh farm cheese and other "Dutch" dishes, such as wienerschnitzel and hot slaw, were on the menu alongside more American fare like "Mignon, Kentucky Country Ham and Fried Chicken dinners." There was also a melted American cheese, fried tomato, onion and bacon sandwich known as a "Bruddy Curran," supposedly named for a regular who had invented it. A 1983 *Louisville Magazine* review said that "Grandfather Bauer favored Kentucky's country cooking," explaining why country ham, fried chicken and Kentucky Bibb lettuce salad were on Bauer's menu for years. The restaurant also offered a lighter soup-and-sandwich lunch menu, echoing the first service at the smithy. In good weather, many people enjoyed their meals on Bauer's patio, shaded by trees growing on the property since smithy days.

By the late 1970s and early 1980s, Bauer's had become the epicenter for what were being called "preppies"—the sort of people who wore madras plaid and seersucker, ached with anticipation over the latest L.L. Bean catalogue or Lilly Pulitzer line and acted as if they had gone to prep school (though it must be said that many Bauer's regulars had actually done so). *The Official Preppy Handbook* of 1980 declared Bauer's "the #1 Prep headquarters in Louisville," advising readers that the Topsiders started really stepping in "after 9:30." Charles F. "Skee" Bauer Jr. told *Louisville Magazine*'s Agnes

Crume that he was amused by the designation but admitted it helped Bauer's get a "younger clientele on weekends, especially on Friday nights." The restaurant had added "continental" dishes, such as "Coquille St. Jacques, shrimp Creole and sole Florentine," to the menu to expand its appeal, but Bauer admitted to the *Highland Herald* in 1983 that he was a bit worried about the "influx of new restaurants" and the interstate highway offering "easy by-pass for potential customers."

In 1984, Bauer got another worry—fire. The two-alarm blaze, possibly set by an arsonist, caused major damage. The kitchen was gutted, antique cabinets and art were destroyed and several rooms sustained smoke damage. The wooden bar, except for a shattered mirror, was spared. The fire closed the restaurant, and regulars wondered if it would ever reopen. A *Courier-Journal* article reported that Trudie Smith of Prospect was particularly worried because Bauer's "was like a private club, really, for everybody in this area. All the waiters knew you by name. You never had to order a drink because the bartender always knew what you wanted and delivered it to you. You almost always sat at the same place."

The Bauers remodeled and reopened. The renovated main dining room was described in *Dining in Historic Kentucky* as "formal, with a pink marble fireplace, Queen Anne–style armchairs, colorful bird wallpaper, and huge brass chandeliers." Though they bounced back from the fire, the Bauers still faced growing competition from area restaurants. And, after over one hundred years in the business, the family may have been growing tired. By 1990, critic Robin Garr had downgraded Bauer's to two and a half stars, saying, "The relaxed, country-club atmosphere and superior service didn't go far enough to make up for second-rate food." Garr described "dry, stringy and fishy salmon, overcooked quail with a Wonder Bread dressing and too-salty sauce; [and] a rib-eye steak sandwich as thin as shoe leather and almost as tough." Garr did enjoy his "Mexican egg rolls stuffed with Monterey Jack cheese" and "Heath Bar crunch pie," however.

The Bauer family handed the restaurant off to others, and the site became La Paloma and then Azalea before closing in 2007. Many of Bauer's "preppy" regulars who had stuck with their "private club" through most of it were very unhappy with what came next: the Bauers decided to sell the property to a national drugstore chain.

As the Bauers asked for permission to raze the property so a Rite-Aid could be built, angry neighbors organized to stop them. Drugstore opponents sought a designation from the Landmarks Commission. The president of the Mockingbird Gardens Neighborhood Association noted, "People…

[were] emotionally attached for the times they have been at the restaurant." The Rolling Fields mayor had "never seen such an outcry over a proposed development." The designation was granted, Rite-Aid went away and the property sat vacant, awaiting a solution both the Bauers and the upper-crust community they had served could both live with. Finally, in 2013, an answer was found. The "designated landmark" was torn down, to be replaced by Mesh, an Indianapolis-based corporate restaurant.

There are new subdivisions, new businesses and new traffic problems on Brownsboro Road where the old smithy once stood. But there is no neon sign announcing fine food "since 1870," and many East End Louisvillians still have a small, vacant space in their hearts where Bauer's used to be.

Chapter 3

CUSCADEN'S

Ice Cream Is "a Food"

History doesn't record who first enjoyed ice cream. Romans ate snow laced with fruit juices, cream and honey, and other cultures, including the Chinese, experienced the pleasures of sweetened, creamy iced treats. By the 1700s, the idea of ice cream had spread throughout Europe, though it was usually reserved for royalty and warmer months. By the mid-1800s, the Industrial Revolution and insulated icehouses began to change things. In Baltimore, dairyman Jacob Fussel became the first mass producer of the frozen confection. But he wasn't the man who became known as the "Ice Cream King." That was George W. Cuscaden, and he earned his crown in Louisville.

After arriving in Louisville from Cincinnati in 1866, Cuscaden and his mother opened a small confectionery on Market Street between Eighth and Ninth, where they cranked out gallons of ice cream a day by hand. It was available only during the summer months and was eaten on site.

Cuscaden, who had a passion for ice cream and quite possibly a hatred of hand-cranking, eagerly explored the new ice cream-making machinery and its possibilities. He decided he could improve them both. In 1875, Cuscaden opened an "ice cream depot," using some of the earliest ice cream–making machinery and marketing to a bewildered public the idea that ice cream could be an easily obtainable, year-round treat. (One slogan was "Ice Cream. It's a food.")

Cuscaden invested early in trucks, kiosks, signage and other methods of marketing his frozen delight for every month. In 1899, he patented a machine that could create a single ice cream brick with four different

The third Cuscaden's Happyland. *Courtesy of University of Louisville.*

colors and flavors. The varicolored bricks became quite popular, and the Ice Cream King opened several ice cream works in Louisville, Cincinnati and Indianapolis. He also operated a number of ice cream parlors in downtown Louisville.

By 1922, Cuscaden was hailed by the Louisville Board of Trade as "the first man to ship ice cream on railroads and one of the very first to sell ice cream soda water." The next time you see a block of Neapolitan or have a root beer float, remember the confectioner who became the Ice Cream King from a little shop on Market Street.

Chapter 4

MAZZONI'S

Oyster Rush Over, Rolled Oysters Remain

By the 1880s, with the Civil War behind it, Louisville was once again a booming river town. Steamships could rapidly make their way from the East Coast and the Gulf of Mexico. The boats brought together two things that created a Louisville food icon: Italian immigrants and the oyster.

In 1884, five Mazzoni brothers arrived in Louisville from Genoa, Italy. According to Greg Haner, a fifth-generation Louisville Mazzoni, the brothers opened taverns in various locations, but Philip Mazzoni's on Third and Market Streets was the one that lasted. Like most taverns of the period, Haner says Mazzoni's was "pretty much a liquor establishment." But to keep patrons drinking, taverns would offer a snack like "a frankfurter…[or] a boiled egg." They would also offer oysters, which, by the 1880s, had become cheap and plentiful through commercial cultivation. Barrels of oysters packed in ice could arrive in Louisville in what seemed like an instant. Oysters were enjoyed at every meal, by rich and poor alike. They were stewed, souped, slurped raw, scalloped, baked, roasted and fried. But at Mazzoni's, they were "rolled."

Marion Flexner called rolled oysters "a distinctive Louisville culinary invention" but inserted a bit of controversy over their origin in her 1949 cookbook. It seems Al Kolb of Kolb's Tavern claimed *his* family invented the rolled oyster, bringing the recipe "to Louisville from New Orleans." But Flexner thought the Mazzonis had a more believable account: "Mazzoni's story is that back in the 1870's a Frenchman who ran a tavern on Third Street had a batch of oysters left over. Not knowing what to do with them, he had one of the cooks whip up a flour and water batter and mix the oysters

Mazzoni's, home of the rolled oyster. *Courtesy of John Nation.*

in this. Then, because they were so small, three or four were rolled together in cracker meal to make one gigantic croquette."

The oysters rolled at Mazzoni's were not simply leftovers for long. According to Haner, the oysters were first dipped in a mix of "oyster liquor, some spices and flour" before being rolled in cracker meal. Deep-frying bursts the fresh oysters, their liquor giving the entire bready inside a mild, pleasant oyster flavor. The combination of cracker crumbs and what the family calls "pastinga" coating kept the fist-sized, salty Mazzoni's rolled oysters a popular item—even when, during Prohibition, the tavern was forced to begin charging five cents for them.

Once repeal came, Mazzoni's found itself owning an original Louisville dish and decided to continue on as a restaurant. As the years went by, Mazzoni's expanded into more locations, with family members operating oyster restaurants from the West End to the Highlands. With the passing of generations, as Haner says, "the ecosystem got messed up," and oysters, once a plentiful item, became more expensive. Mazzoni's left downtown in 1989 after 105 years, citing changes in dietary habits and "nearly nonexistent" evening customers. It managed to stay open on Taylorsville Road across from Bowman Field for three decades and then moved to Middletown in 2007 before closing a year later.

Mazzoni's lives on in the rolled oyster, still found at a number of local restaurants. But to Haner, one of the last of the Mazzoni line to have sold rolled oysters in Louisville, they may not be the same. "There's an art to the rolling technique," he told the Southern Foodways Alliance. "You don't want it to be heavy so…you need to sort of flip it around in your hand without touching it too many times and then give it a final press which encrusts those oysters inside… [and] if you have an oyster out it just blows out the side and you can't serve it."

A recipe is provided for those wishing to see if they can re-create the famous Mazzoni's rolled oyster. Have some beer handy and, perhaps, as Flexner recommended, some "catsup in a small bowl with a teaspoon of very hot brown mustard to top it." That's Louisville style.

Rolled Oysters

Adapted from Marion Flexner's *Out of Kentucky Kitchens*. Makes six rolls.

Mazzoni's method was to "dry" the oysters with a light coating of cracker crumbs, then dip them in the "pastinga" and then cover again with cracker crumbs. Flexner recommended dipping the oysters first in batter, then rolling in meal and then repeating the process. But Mary McCauley, a longtime Mazzoni's oyster roller, told the Louisville Times *in 1985 that the oysters "can't be redipped." According to McCauley, "If you redip them, they get tough. It's a one-shot deal." So while the recipe below is mostly based on Flexner's, it uses Mazzoni's dipping method.*

> *18 small- to medium-sized oysters*
> *about 5 ounces oyster crackers*
> *salt and pepper*
> *½ cup flour*
> *1 teaspoon baking powder*
> *¼ teaspoon salt*
> *¼ cup milk*
> *1 large egg*
> *vegetable oil or lard for frying*

Drain oysters, reserving their liquor.

In a food processor, process oyster crackers into a fine meal. Place meal in a shallow bowl and season generously with pepper. Add salt to taste. (Crackers may be salty, so be careful.)

Working a few at a time, place oysters in the cracker meal and toss to cover. Lay coated oysters on a sheet of waxed paper, letting them dry a bit while preparing the other ingredients.

Sift flour, baking powder and ¼ teaspoon salt into a medium-sized mixing bowl. In a small bowl, whisk the milk, egg and 2 tablespoons of reserved oyster liquor together. Add milk mixture to flour mixture to make a stiff batter.

Add the meal-covered oysters, six at a time, to the batter. Take three batter-covered oysters out and form them into a croquette. Working quickly, roll them in seasoned cracker meal, covering completely. Lay the croquette on waxed paper. Repeat the process until all oysters are used and six croquettes are made.

Heat several inches of oil or lard in a small saucepan. When the oil reaches 350 degrees, drop in a croquette using a slotted spoon. Then, drop in another. Fry, two at a time, turning with a slotted spoon as needed until browned on all sides. Drain on a rack or on paper towels.

Serve with tartar sauce or, as Flexner suggested, with catsup and hot mustard.

Chapter 5

VIENNA

Rescued by Democrats, Ruined by Fire

In 1958, Louisvillians could still see the flamboyant exterior of the Vienna Restaurant in the 100 block of South Fourth. Barry Bingham Sr., patriarch of a Louisville media empire, penned a description in his newspaper that year, recalling a childhood lunch with his father in 1912 or 1913.

Bingham wrote that, around the turn of the twentieth century, the Vienna Restaurant and Bakery was "the favored rendezvous" of Louisvillians whose "epicurean tastes…recognized its superiority in fittings, service and fare." Opened in another building in 1893 by Frank Erpeldinger ("from the fine old town of Coblenz on the Rhine"), the Vienna ruled Louisville's restaurant scene until 1927. Bingham claimed Erpeldinger first called his Fourth Street establishment the "Chicago Restaurant" before it became celebrated as the Vienna. But during World War I, when "peculiar semantic foolishness" caused "German measles" to become "liberty measles," Erpeldinger changed the name to the Model Bakery and Restaurant—though "everybody went on calling it the Vienna all the same."

The 1903 building's polychrome exterior, which reminded Bingham of "the witch's house in 'Hansel and Gretel,' a structure built of cake and candy," was actually terra cotta turned out by Cincinnati's Rookwood Pottery, one of the first American potteries to gain international recognition. The National Park Service's Historic Buildings Survey described the building as "a very rare example of the Art Nouveau influence in Louisville." The interior was exuberant as well, covered with decorative tiles. The kitchen and bakery were on the second floor and "fancy pastry" on the third.

Vienna Restaurant building, 1970s. *Courtesy of Library of Congress.*

In Bingham's mind's eye, there were "snowy linen[s], large napkins folded in fancy patterns, [and] the subdued gleam of cutlery and glass," as well as a "succession of old-fashioned fans turning their broad, brown wooden blades in the ceiling." He recalled meeting "various elderly gents with mustaches, high stiff collars and gold watch chains." One of them could have been Erpeldinger himself, as a photograph of Frank shows a stiff-collared, steely-eyed man with a rather impressive Teutonic mustache.

Bingham's childhood lunchtime menu featured "many dishes of the sustaining German or Austrian kind," with a special highlight being "Vienna rolls, a whole battery of them, some decked with caraway seeds." These rolls, also known as Kaiser rolls (something that might have been downplayed during the "semantic foolishness"), have a thin, slightly crisp crust and a distinctive star pattern on top. A Vienna Restaurant recipe appears in Marion Flexner's *Out of Kentucky Kitchens*. It calls for a veal roast ("cut from the leg"), a can of anchovy fillets and "1 or 2 veal kidneys, depending on the size of the roast." Flexner advised readers to let their butchers assemble the meat. This may have been easier for Flexner, whose cookbook was originally published in 1949. When she talked to her butcher about the preparation, he haughtily replied, "You don't have to tell me how to prepare that—I used to do it for the Old Vienna!"

Described by Bingham as "the haunt of the most prominent merchants and professional men," the Vienna's reputation grew so formidable that Erpeldinger could afford to offend patrons. One tale involved a customer complaining about poor service and asking Erpeldinger to have one of his sixty employees fired. "Hell, sir," Erpeldinger supposedly responded, "waiters are harder to get than customers."

Erpeldinger died in 1927, leaving a niece to run the restaurant for a few years before selling to a Chicago outfit, which closed it not long after. (The Great Depression, which began in 1929, may have been a factor.) In 1951, the building was taken over by the Jefferson County Democratic Party. In 1959, a fire swept through the building, destroying the wood and tile interior and sending "a blast of fire" through the Rookwood front. It was still standing in the late 1970s, however, when included in the Historic Buildings Survey. But now, where the Vienna's glorious façade once stood, is a bland, beige parking structure.

In 1958, Bingham Sr. was wondering if the Vienna's time had passed. He noted that, by the 1920s, when the restaurant closed, "women, and men too, were beginning to watch their diets and were shunning heavy foods." The Vienna was "based on the European theory that people have time to talk and enjoy their food"—something that seemed incredible to his busy mid-century eyes. Still, almost a generation later, Frank Erpeldinger's Vienna was being remembered for owning "the look of comfort, the atmosphere of calm good service, and the savor of fine food that is the eternal hallmark of a good eating house."

Chapter 6

MILLER'S

Nearly One Hundred Years of Home Cooking

Mr. and Mrs. Rudolph Miller may not have understood the significance of the house they bought in 1898. The couple was just looking for a place to live and some extra income. Mrs. Miller recalled in a newspaper article that the "enormous old house" at 429 South Second Street had "24 rooms, including the back part that was separate from the main house." The "back part," dating from the 1830s, had actually been used as slaves' quarters. Along with 432 South Fifth Street (which became the Old House Restaurant), it is now one of the last surviving antebellum homes in downtown Louisville. To the Millers, it was the perfect place for a boardinghouse.

The Millers began taking in boarders, providing them with family-style meals. Then one morning around the start of the twentieth century, Mrs. Miller answered a knock on her door. A student from the medical university nearby was there, and as Mrs. Miller recalled, "asked if we would be willing to give meals to about 25 medical and dental students." They agreed, and a restaurant began. The first meals at Miller's were served "home style," with "platters of meat, bowls of vegetables and heaping plates of hot biscuits" passed around the table at fifteen cents a head. As the audience continued to expand, the Millers replaced the wood- and coal-fired ranges with electric stoves, installed steam tables and began cafeteria-style service. Miller's had a free soundtrack, with the Christ Church Cathedral on one side and the Sisters of Mercy on the other.

The popularity of Miller's grew during the 1937 flood, when the restaurant was spared the water that inundated most of downtown.

Site of Miller's Cafeteria. *Michelle Turner.*

Martha Goheen, a descendant of the Millers who took over the restaurant in the 1980s, told the *Highland Herald*, "During the flood of '37....my parents prepared food for the civil service workers and distributed it in 50-gallon cans." Goheen's parents, Rudolph Miller Jr. and his wife, Beatrice, took over the restaurant's operations in the 1930s, although the original Mrs. Miller stayed on in an "active" role. She lived in a second-floor apartment in the old house and said that she enjoyed being on hand "to keep an eye on things."

A 1954 advertisement touted Miller's as the place to go "for a huge variety of home-cooked food" and promised that "the atmosphere…[left] nothing to be desired." Eggplant casserole, chicken livers and salmon croquettes with white sauce and green peas were found on Miller's cafeteria line. Louisvillians of all stripes favored Miller's, as the family reported seeing "Mercedes and LG&E trucks" sitting side-by-side in the parking lot. Attorneys from downtown law firms made Miller's a regular lunch stop, passing the tradition down to their associates.

Mrs. Miller died in 1958 at the age of ninety-four in the home she moved into in 1898. Rudolph Jr. kept the restaurant going through the 1960s, when urban renewal projects began eradicating much of the neighborhood. As people were leaving the downtown area, Miller's faced its "hardest times," but people kept coming. Lunch crowds were still eating Miller's "basic American food" until 1998, when the Goheens closed the cafeteria.

The cathedral next door acquired the property around 2000. In 2004, the cafeteria extension was demolished, and "stabilization measures" were undertaken to restore what was being called the "Howard-Hardy" house by the National Register of Historic Places. First called "Cathedral Commons," the restored property debuted as an apartment building, which was lauded for its successful completion. However, the project was unsuccessful and, in 2011, became vacant. In 2014, a law firm bought the house, telling the *Courier-Journal* they were attracted to its "long staircase" and "long hallways"—and perhaps, the faint echoes of other attorneys who had shared war stories over salmon croquettes.

Chapter 7

BENEDICT'S

Spending Immortality as a Spread

Few who have visited Louisville, especially around Derby time, have failed to sample Benedictine, a cucumber and cream cheese spread. It was created by Jennie C. Benedict, perhaps Louisville's most famous cook.

Benedict was born at Harrods Creek in 1860, where her family had a wholesale business in molasses and other staples. As a child, she cooked in the family kitchen and talked of either becoming a missionary or someone who catered. While Benedict did devote a good portion of her life to charity, catering came first. In her 1904 publication of *The Blue Ribbon Cook Book*, Benedict told those "seeking suggestion or advice as to how to take up the work as I did" that "social duties must be abandoned" because the business of catering required one to work "early and late, giving everything up absolutely." The 1904 edition was the second release of the book subtitled *One Hundred Tested Receipts, Together With Others Which Have Been Tried and Found Valuable*. Benedict released the first edition in 1897 "at the request of many" for her recipes, but not before the canny businesswoman had "subscriptions enough to pay for the complete edition."

The subscription strategy was not the first marketing tool Benedict employed to build her catering business. She began in 1893 behind her home at Third and Ormsby, taking a $381 loan with a local contractor in order to build a kitchen. Within six months, solely from making fruitcakes, Benedict paid off her debt and then decided to branch out. She gained customers by distributing five hundred circulars promising to deliver anything "from a cup of chocolate to furnishing and serving a large reception." Her work attracted the attention of two high school principals, who realized "the great advantage of having lunches properly prepared for the pupils," and asked Benedict to supply them. Also impressed were the publishers of the *Courier-Journal*, who soon made Benedict the editor of the newspaper's household department.

Not long after, at a "Pure Food Exhibition" held in Louisville, Benedict was asked to fill in for a representative of the Boston Cooking School made famous by Fannie Farmer who, "owing to severe illness," was unable to carry out her duties. Benedict substituted so admirably that it "opened the doors and hearts" of the culinary institution, and Benedict "entered the school the following winter, under the most favorable circumstances, and took a special course." It was at the school, Benedict wrote, where she found her "inspiration for higher things."

After returning to Louisville, Benedict "went to work in earnest, determined to strive for the topmost round of the ladder." She traveled the state conducting cooking classes, taught others at her home and continued to build her catering business. In her introduction to the 2008 reprinting of *The Blue Ribbon Cook Book*, Susan Reigler related how Benedict's creations "became the centerpieces" of parties for Louisville's "most prominent citizens," especially during Derby season. People clamored for her fruitcakes, beaten biscuits, plum puddings, chicken salad and angel food cake. And, of course, there was Benedictine.

Not to be confused with the liqueur or the monastic order, Benedictine is a smooth, slightly tangy spread made primarily from cucumber juice and cream cheese. These days, people use it as a dip or enjoy it with bacon in a sandwich, but in Miss Jennie's time, Benedictine was usually served on crustless soft white bread as part of a teatime assortment. Where Benedictine does not appear, however, is in Benedict's cookbook. Reigler wrote that the recipe, for which Benedict "is almost exclusively remembered today," is not in any of the multiple editions of her cookbook. Why Benedict left the eponymous creation out is a question no one has ever been able to answer.

In 1900, Benedict opened a restaurant and tearoom at 412 South Fourth Street. A 1907 advertisement "cordially invited" the public to a "fall importations" opening, promising "unusually beautiful novelties in baskets and boxes" and "cotillion favors and souvenirs."

By 1911, Miss Jennie's business and reputation had grown so large that Benedict's reopened at a roomier location at 554 South Fourth. A stunning feature was a soda fountain made from rocks taken from Mammoth Cave. Each end of the fountain was open to represent a small cave, with red lights

Benedict's, circa 1924. *Courtesy of University of Louisville.*

emanating from the artificial caverns. Modern conveniences such as electric lighting and fans and "dainty accessories that are so pleasing and gratifying to the eye" made Benedict's tearoom quite a popular gathering place. Young people especially seemed to enjoy Benedict's, leading Miss Jennie to quip that she may have been "the repository of more lovers' confidence than any other woman in Louisville."

The restaurant served a wide variety of dishes, ranging from dainty ("Grape Fruit Cocktail," "Consomme, plain" and "Banana Sliced in Cream") to hearty ("Pork Chops [2] with Fried Apples," all manner of steaks and seafood and no fewer than nine different potato preparations). Preserves and relishes were available "a'la carte." Desserts included Peach Melba and Baked Alaska.

Just before World War I, Miss Jennie catered a society wedding in St. Louis that so impressed that city's elite they offered a guarantee of $1 million in business within three years if she would move there. That's when Louisvillians launched the movement "to keep Miss Jennie at home." In an unprecedented move, a committee presented her with a letter saying,

"Louisville can ill afford to lose a citizen like you, one who has always been a leader in every civic and social movement and who has always stood for the advancement of its commercial interests. The name of Jennie C. Benedict & Co. has radiated to all parts of our country the name of Louisville." Benedict said "so great was the pressure brought to bear that…[she] promptly abandoned the thought of even considering such a move."

Miss Jennie continued operating her business until retiring in 1925. Benedict's continued on for several years after and was still quite popular. Groucho Marx visited in 1927 with R.G. Potter, the salesman and photographer who collected and created many of Louisville's iconic images.

After she sold the business, Benedict retired to a house she named "Indianola" on a property called "Dream Acre," overlooking the Ohio River from a bluff above Mellwood Avenue. She wrote an autobiography called *Road to Dream Acre*, published in 1928, the same year she died. It does not include a recipe for Benedictine. A historical marker was erected in Old Louisville, where her catering business began. The marker named Benedict as a "chef, caterer and author," noted her work as "a social reformer for the women and the poor" and, of course, her creation of Benedictine, "a sandwich spread that remains a Kentucky food specialty." Like Benedict herself, however, the marker does not provide a recipe.

Luncheon Rolls

Adapted from Jennie Benedict's *Blue Ribbon Cook Book*. Makes about twelve rolls.

Benedict's rather mystifying recipe indicated neither oven temperature nor flour amount nor rising time. We modified the recipe to make something much like Louisville's beloved Camelot Buns, which are perfect for serving with beef tenderloin and Henry Bain sauce. We think Miss Jennie would approve.

> ½ cup scalded milk
> 2 tablespoons sugar
> ¼ teaspoon salt
> 1⅛ teaspoons active dry yeast
> about 2¼ cups flour
> 2 tablespoons melted butter, with a bit extra for brushing
> 1 egg and 1 egg yolk, well beaten

To hot milk, add sugar and salt; dissolve in yeast when milk has cooled to just lukewarm. Stir in ¾ cup of flour, cover and let rise for 30 minutes or until bubbly. Add melted butter and beaten eggs, then enough flour to form a slightly sticky dough ball. Knead (by hand or in a stand mixer) for about 3 minutes, then cover and let rise again until doubled in bulk.

Roll out dough to about ⅛ inch thickness, then cut into approximately 2-inch rounds. Place half of the rounds in a buttered baking pan. Brush with melted butter, then place remaining rounds on top. Cover and let the rounds rise again until just about doubled in height.

Brush the tops with butter, then bake in a 375-degree oven for about 10 minutes until golden brown.

Chapter 8

SENNING'S

Successfully Following Streetcars to South Louisville

Carl Frederick Senning arrived in Louisville from Germany in 1868. In 1877, he married Minnie Goeper, and the couple purchased their first restaurant in downtown Louisville, opening a second five years later. Louisville's streetcar lines were stretching southward to Frederick Law Olmsted's Iroquois Park, and the innovative Sennings (said to have introduced finger bowls and bowling alleys to Louisville) saw opportunity at that end of the compass.

In 1902, the couple built Senning's Park, which served as both their home and a restaurant/beer garden. Senning's Park was an early addition to the South End's once-strong beer garden scene. Beer gardens had long been popular with Louisville's large German immigrant population. As *The Encyclopedia of Louisville* explains: "These establishments catered to families, not just male drinkers, and Sunday was by far their biggest business day, since it was the only day most people were off work. In the summer beer gardens sold two to five times as much beer on Sunday as the rest of the week put together."

In the 1920s, Carl and Minnie's son, William, took over the family business, adding what became Louisville's first zoo. In a 2013 *LEO Weekly* interview, ninety-four-year-old Edith Hatfield remembered dates taking her in the 1930s to Senning's Park, where she "used to dance the night away" to "all the big bands [playing] there."

The expansive space and availability of beer made Senning's a popular political dinner spot. Six Kentucky governors received their nominations

Senning's Park postcard. *Courtesy of University of Louisville.*

from the beer garden's gazebo. Senning's was so popular that additional streetcars had to be added to the Third and New Cut Road line. In its heyday, crowds of eight to ten thousand people were reported.

The park survived the Great Depression, but in 1939, the enterprise was sold. Renamed Colonial Bar and Grill, the 1940s-era park echoed with the sounds of big-band entertainment and dancing feet. In the 1950s, it transformed again, becoming known as the Teen Bar, a strictly nonalcoholic venue so popular with South End teenagers that it had its own newsletter. A popular jitterbug contest, held on Wednesday evenings, was hosted by local TV and radio personality Ed Kallay. Changing again to Colonial Gardens in the late 1950s, the space changed hands several times, shifting from pop to country to karaoke.

Despite the series of owners' best efforts, Colonial Gardens was closed in June 2003. In 2008, Senning's Park was put up for historic designation, with advocates claiming the property marked "the cultural response to the transformation of roads and travel modes in the late-nineteenth and early-twentieth century." The designation was granted, and in 2013, Mayor Greg Fischer indicated that the city would buy the property. In 2014, Fischer announced a partnership with developer Underhill Associates, which is exploring possibilities for Colonial Gardens. Their ideas include family-oriented restaurants and an ice cream shop. There are also plans for a beer garden, where perhaps future governors will be nominated. (No zoo, however. Louisville already has one.)

Chapter 9

KUNZ'S

Flying "The Dutchman" Around Downtown

The mention of Kunz's in any gathering of Louisvillians may release a flood of memories, as well as heated arguments over how long the restaurant lasted and where it may have been. "Louisville's Oldest Downtown Restaurant" stayed within the boundaries of the business district. But surviving for over a century required both good food and good business sense—qualities the Kunz family possessed for generations.

Jacob Kunz arrived in Louisville in 1885. Born in Indiana at the start of the Civil War, the twenty-four-year-old Kunz came to Kentucky to work for a liquor wholesaler. Seven years later, in 1892, he opened his own firm, J. Kunz & Co., supplying wine and liquor to Louisville from 440 West Market Street. A group of businessmen started to hang around Kunz's establishment, forming a group they called the "Peach Tree Club," and began to demand more than drink from Jacob Kunz, who obliged by offering cheese and crackers.

The food grew to be as popular as the wine and liquor, and in 1903, Kunz & Co. made its first move, to West Market. According to *A Sesqui-Centennial History of Kentucky*, Kunz began offering "a complete line of Fancy Groceries" and a delicatessen with "buffet service and private dining rooms in addition to the regular wine and liquor service." In 1907, Kunz moved the business to Second Street, where despite (or possibly because of) Prohibition, the food and beverage provider's reputation continued to grow. Jacob Kunz died in 1927, leaving the family's reputation and business in the hands of his three sons. In 1933, after the repeal of Prohibition, the Kunz brothers

Kunz's, with its "quaint Dutch motif." *Courtesy of University of Louisville.*

moved once again, this time to 608 South Fourth in a facility decorated with what a menu described as a "quaint Dutch motif."

In 1941, at the beginning of World War II, Kunz & Co. moved to a larger space at 619 South Fourth. Kunz's prominence kept growing in the postwar years. The spacious restaurant advertised several dining areas, including the "Cozy Luncheon Room, the Coffee Shop, the Main Dining Room, the Business Men's Nook on the balcony, and the Quality Candy Department." Keith Runyon, former editor of the *Courier-Journal*, recalled in a letter to *Louisville Magazine* that the restaurant "was very Germanic inside, a reminder of Louisville's Teutonic heritage, and near the entrance there was a large model windmill that actually turned. The whole place was decorated with large beer steins and smelled faintly of vinegar." In this period, Kunz's claimed it offered menus "equal to every mood, taste and preference—savory snacks, breakfasts, luncheons or full meals for the individual family or dinner party." It promised that "satisfying meals based on quality ingredients and better cookery shall ALWAYS be the first consideration."

J. Kunz & Co.'s the Dutchman, at 619 South Fourth Street, with a picture of Jacob Kunz. *Courtesy of University of Louisville.*

Kunz's, 1949. *Courtesy of University of Louisville.*

Kunz's the Dutchman, 526 South Fourth Street, 1960s. *Courtesy of University of Louisville.*

In 1962, Kunz's the Dutchman opened in a new location on Fourth, by then called an "avenue" instead of a "street." Kunz's promenade traded the mid-century neon of the 600 block for a gleaming copper hood at 526 Fourth Avenue. The interior décor reflected the copper hood's 1960s exuberance. A 1962 article in *Louisville à la Carte!* gushed, "The carpeted circular stairway leads to the second floor Carnival Room. Across from the stairway is a tall, gold pier mirror, which was salvaged from a Louisville home. Hanging from the ceiling is a chandelier from a French castle via New Orleans." The photo spread caught a "curved fruitwood wainscoting and massive balustrade" separating a lounge from "the Kunz Room," which was "carpeted in a custom made Bigelow that is a color reverse of the gold and damask wallpaper used in the dining room" under more imported French chandeliers. A gallery featured "smoke finished, distressed mirrors" and a door into the adjoining Byck's, through which models from the women's apparel shop entered on Mondays to "put on informal style shows."

Even as the downtown business district suffered decay and through the foot-traffic-only period of the "River City Mall," the Dutchman kept going. Through the 1960s, '70s and '80s, Kunz's was known for its "famous

Dutchman steaks, Chateaubriand…wiener schnitzel, seafood, pork chops and baby barbecued ribs." The restaurant advertised its "prized collection of beer steins lend[ing] authentic charm to the popular Peach Tree Lounge." In 1983, *Louisville Skyline* reported that Kunz's was "an immensely popular lunch and dinner spot," attracting businesspeople at lunch and "theater and concert goers, conventioneers, as well as loyal, regular customers at dinner." However, John Kunz admitted that the Galleria's restaurants had "put a small dint in…[the] lunch trade," and a new, cheaper menu was being rolled out.

In 1987, the Kunz family opened another establishment a few blocks north called Kunz's Fourth & Market on the ground floor of a state-owned parking garage. Smaller, yet seating more people than the venerable copper-fronted flagship, the new location proved popular. And while Fred Kunz initially claimed the family would operate both locations, by 1988, things had changed. At the start of that year, the announcement came that the Dutchman would be shutting down—something Fred Kunz finally acknowledged had always been part of the plan. The new restaurant, at 115 Fourth Avenue, was close to downtown hotels and attractions. The Dutchman, on the other hand, was described by the *Courier-Journal* as "a decaying building in an area that…[was] largely deserted after dark" and had not "been redecorated in 15 years."

On Saturday, January 23, 1988, according to the *Courier-Journal*, "elegantly dressed diners marked the end" of the Dutchman's "55-year reign…as a culinary landmark." The bar stayed open until 2:00 a.m. Sunday, with many people remaining for another hour "to share memories and stretch out the establishment's final moments." Not long after that, a fire began.

The three-alarm blaze destroyed the entire building. A witness said it was "like a pit of fire," with flames "coming out of the center." The main part of the building completely collapsed, and the famous copper hood façade was removed by the fire department over fears of it "spattering debris into the sidewalk and street." Fred Kunz, who arrived at the fire "still wearing his white shirt, gray suit and topcoat," saw the building burn, along with its collection of beer steins and irreplaceable family photographs.

The total loss of the Dutchman and its memorabilia meant Kunz's Fourth & Market could never replicate the "quaint Dutch motif" and ambience of the prior locations. Nor did the food garner the praise it had in earlier eras. The *1989–90 Scene Dining Guide* praised Fourth & Market's "elegant" look, but noted, "Lately the food…hasn't matched the setting. It wasn't badly prepared, just uninspired." Still, the private dining and convention-related business grew. In 1996, Kunz's negotiated for more space. The restaurant continued operating for another decade, but "Louisville's Oldest Downtown Restaurant" closed in 2007 after a bankruptcy filing, when "utility service was on the verge of being shut off."

In 2009, a new restaurant (Z's Fusion) opened in the Fourth & Market space, completely erasing any Teutonic traces of J. Kunz & Co. from Market Street, where the dynasty began. These days, when walking down a revitalized Fourth Street, the only trace of Kunz's left in Louisville is a faint outline of the old Dutchman building—an imprint from the 1988 fire.

Chapter 10

COLONNADE

Innovative Service and Unforgettable Pies

C afeterias began around the dawn of the twentieth century and quickly spread throughout America, offering food people could see in clean, comfortable environments that welcomed women as well as men. As they grew in popularity, most cafeterias set up their restaurants along a similar pattern. Customers obtained trays, napkins and silverware at one end of a serving line, pushed their trays past desserts (owners found putting them first increased sales), salads, sides and main dishes and then paid for their selections. Seeing the growth of the cafeteria trade around 1900, Roland W. White, a chemist and engineer who had become a successful developer, decided he would get into the business. White had definite opinions. His Colonnade Cafeterias stressed cleanliness and quick service and created a different kind of system. White opened the first Colonnade in Cleveland in 1911, the same year John Price Starks commissioned architects from Chicago to design a building for his "growing retail concern" in Louisville. When the Beaux-Arts building opened in 1913, a Colonnade Cafeteria was downtown a few blocks away. In 1926, the Colonnade moved into the Starks Building basement, and a Louisville tradition was born.

The Colonnade chain quickly established a reputation for what Duncan Hines called "wholesome food prepared by competent women cooks in immaculate kitchens." White's "thoroughly systematized" ideas of the function and administration of cafeterias were declared by the American Dietetic Association in 1920 to be "far in advance of most people's ideas on the subject." There were hot meats, sandwiches, pies,

The Starks Building stairway to the Colonnade Cafeteria. *Courtesy of University of Louisville.*

breads and desserts. But instead of following a single line, patrons could begin at whatever station they chose, moving between salads, sandwiches and steam tables in whichever manner they felt moved to do. Colonnade workers rewarded tray-laden patrons with a receipt recording their choices, which would be tendered at a cashier station after eating. This "free square style" supposedly offered customers the ability to get what they desired with less waiting.

Though White died in 1953, the Colonnade Company kept on reinforcing his principles with "circular letters," memoranda detailing menu variations, cost control suggestions, charity events and, embarrassingly to modern eyes, how to handle minorities. Louisville's Filson Historical Society featured several Colonnade "circulars" in a blog post titled "Behind the Scenes of Segregation in Louisville." An April 1952 missive dealt with "Public Relations—Appearance of Guests." Colonnade workers were reminded that they could refuse service to patrons in "overalls or soiled work clothes" and "men or women in shorts or otherwise scantily clad." While this may seem like a somewhat stricter version of "no shirt, no shoes, no service," the next memo, titled "Public Relations—Undesirable Guests," makes things clearer. Quoting the Thirteenth Amendment and noting the rise of equal access laws, the circular reminded staff that public accommodations could be refused "as long as they were refused 'for reasons applicable to all persons.'"

The company's fears of desegregation were unfounded, as the Colonnade continued to be popular even after its racially tinged policies were discarded and the attraction of the cafeteria concept as a whole began to fade. A restaurant guide from the 1980s described the Colonnade's "appetizing array of over one hundred selections of specially cooked food and pastries" and called out the restaurant's "attractive surroundings with more cheerful service than you expect in a cafeteria." There was always a wide selection of salads, which might include an iceberg wedge with cottage cheese dressing and "chiffonade salad" with its red French dressing mixed with diced hard-boiled eggs, pimento, sweet pickle, parsley and onion. Those wanting a hot lunch could choose from a rotating selection of turkey and dressing, corned beef and cabbage, roast beef, ham and other meats. Sides included macaroni and cheese, southern-style greens and scalloped tomatoes with croutons on top. The sandwich station offered numerous options, including the favorite of many: braunschweiger and Swiss cheese on pumpernickel bread. Desserts were beloved, especially all manner of meringue pies that were also available whole to take home.

The Colonnade became a hangout for lawyers, judges and businessmen, a group of whom had a special large table "reserved" for their consistent patronage. Louisville attorney Greg Haynes recalls that the regulars' table "had stuff lacquered on it, saying it was their table." Haynes reports that the loyalty of one particular lawyer, Larry Jones of the firm Wyatt, Tarrant &

Combs, ran so deep that he left bequests for most of the Colonnade staff in his will.

Like much of Louisville's downtown, the Starks Building began to age. In 1989, a pipe burst directly over the cafeteria, sending thousands of gallons of water into the restaurant just after the lunch rush. However, the Colonnade was quickly repaired and carried on.

In 1996, the Colonnade was purchased by a local partnership. But in 2006, the Starks Building was sold to a new company, which asked the restaurant to leave. The new owners operated various restaurants in town under the Colonnade name. In 2008, there was talk of returning the Colonnade to the Starks Building basement, but those plans never materialized. The building was sold again in 2015, and a major makeover was promised. There is a restaurant operating on the Starks Building street level at this writing. But Roland White's passion for service, the Colonnade's legendary pies and its peculiar serving system are long gone.

Chapter II

CUNNINGHAM'S

Fallen Women, Fish Sandwiches and a Flexible Approach to the Law

James N. "Cap" Cunningham, the man who would contribute the most to the outsized legends of Cunningham's Restaurant, would not be born until decades after the eatery at Fifth and Breckinridge Streets began. In 1870, there were no fish sandwiches, no turtle soup, no aging waiters. There was simply a blacksmith shop and livery stable on the outskirts of the city, owned by a Mr. Melton. He began stocking groceries and created a delicatessen, offering meals and snacks to the carters and coachmen lingering with their livery. Melton soon sold the entire business to one of his meat-cutters, who installed a bar with mammoth mirrors and heavy carved wood supports and began focusing more on food and entertainment. Henry Schultz took over the food-serving smithy in 1906, but soon it was sold again to Joe Insert, referred to in Cunningham's own history as "a man of questionable integrity." It may have been around this time that what would become known as Cunningham's became a bordello.

The upper floors of the stable were said to have been leased to a woman named Mary Polly and her "sisters," who operated a profitable "rooming house." This sort of establishment was not unknown to Louisville, nor rare at the time. An 1895 "sporting guide" for a Grand Army of the Republic reunion lists over twenty-five separate establishments offering "the most beautiful ladies in the South," along with "the choicest brands of Wines and Beer," where "sportively inclined" gentlemen could keep themselves entertained while in Louisville. But this kind of good times wouldn't last forever, as Cap Cunningham incorporated the restaurant into his beat.

Cunningham's, 1926. *Courtesy of University of Louisville.*

Cunningham was a soldier before he became a combination cop and restaurateur. Returning to Louisville from World War I, Cunningham became active in Republican politics, and that led to the Louisville police department, which in pre–civil service days was a purely political creation. By 1920, the first year of Prohibition, Cunningham had risen to captain. In 1922, as the city remained officially dry, he bought the building at 900 South Fifth Street. Molly and her "sisters" were evicted, and Cap opened a restaurant.

The constitutional amendment banning alcohol was not popular in Louisville, and Cap's behavior as he began his restaurant is a good example. In partnership with a man named Joe Coleman, Cunningham's "Soft Drink Stand" became so popular that he briefly opened a second outlet on Third Street—that is, until federal agents found the drinks to be more "hard" than "soft" and closed Cap's business down. Undeterred by this incident, Cunningham kept his food service going until the nation regained its senses. Despite being a staunch Republican, Cunningham grabbed the first beer license made available after FDR's 1932 election. His restaurant became even more popular than during its "soft drink" phase. All signs of the former smithy were erased as Cunningham replaced the stables with private dining rooms and put the enormous bar where the blacksmith once stood. In 1942, Cunningham created Louisville's first "drive-in" restaurant, where waiters would serve drinks and dinners to motorists pulling up to the large parking lot.

As the years went by, Cunningham's became known not only for its racy history but also for its fish sandwiches, its private booths and its long-serving waitstaff. Turtle soup was a big seller, and patrons holed up behind swinging saloon doors could buzz down for a bowl along with beer and (now legal) bourbon drinks. Cunningham's expanded to seat 350 people. Drive-through service remained popular despite other restaurants getting in on the idea during the postwar boom.

In 1967, seventy-five-year-old Cap Cunningham sold his business to four Louisville restaurant owners, including Mrs. Shirley James, owner of Pussy Cat A Go Go. Two years later, in 1969, Cap died of a heart attack while driving on Durret Lane. While keeping the name Cunningham's, Mrs. James and the others sold the restaurant to a new owner in the same year. The operation passed ownership several more times, ending up with the George family in the 1980s.

Cunningham's remained in operation at its original location until 2001, when the former blacksmith shop, brothel and bootlegging operation burned in a fire. The Cunningham name is now attached to a restaurant called "Creekside" in Louisville's far East End. Since the fire, however, at Fifth and Breckinridge Streets, only the memories of shuffling waiters, historic Louisville memorabilia and the ethical issues of policing morality remain.

Chapter 12
LITTLE TAVERN

White Castle? What White Castle?

Ubiquity may make it seem they arrived with the Pilgrims, but hamburgers didn't really become part of America until the twentieth century. By 1927, America had fallen in love with burgers—especially little square ones with steamed onions on top. Expanding rapidly from Kansas, White Castle restaurants were popping up everywhere, offering sacks of five-cent burgers that people couldn't seem to get enough of. And like any successful idea, the gleaming white building with its limited menu spawned a number of imitators. One of the more successful was Little Tavern, founded in Louisville by Harry Duncan.

Duncan was born in Missouri in 1899 and started selling food at fairs and festivals as a teenager. In 1924, he opened the first of his Baby Beef Shops in St. Louis, which quickly grew to five outlets. The next year, White Castle opened its first restaurant in the city. Not long after that, a fortuneteller told Duncan it might be better if he'd "head east." After moving to Louisville, Duncan opened his first Little Tavern at 510 West Broadway. The small, square white building was quite similar to White Castle's design.

Duncan was not the only entrepreneur to see the potential in imitating White Castle. As America warmed to sliders, turrets, towers and other castle-ish restaurant features popped up everywhere. White Palace, White Log, White House, White Tavern and White Hut offered hamburgers, a fast-food carryout style and other similarities. Unsurprisingly, White Castle was not pleased with this eruption of imitators and served up threats and lawsuits along with its steamed little square hamburgers. However, White

Little Tavern No. 6, looking a lot like White Castle. *Courtesy of University of Louisville.*

Castle often helped the imitators by paying for new signs or architecture, allowing them to continue operation without copyright infringement.

It is unclear whether Duncan was assisted by White Castle or even legally threatened by the company. But in Louisville, Duncan opened several other outlets beyond the first West Broadway "castle" before expanding eastward to the Washington, D.C. area in 1928. There, he unveiled a new (less like White Castle) design for Little Tavern. The restaurant prototype was transformed into a "white-painted cottage with a green tile roof illuminated by gooseneck lamps and neon signs." Though he may have remodeled the look of Little Tavern, Duncan did not step away from his "Buy 'em by the Bag" slogan, which was merely a word away from White Castle's "Buy 'em by the Sack."

Little Tavern grew to over fifty locations and, along with Krystal, became one of the South's largest hamburger chains. While the last Louisville Little Tavern location closed in the 1940s, the little shop that wasn't White Castle helped create cravings that still occur around America.

Chapter 13

CHINA INN

"Chop Suey," Cave Hill, Congress and the Cabbage Patch

Chin Ming and his wife arrived in Louisville in the 1920s, taking ownership of buildings downtown that had previously been used for, among other things, meetings and gambling. The property was given to them by Chin Ming's father, Chin Jack Lem. A family history donated to the Kentucky Historical Society says the property, acquired through collection of a debt or some type of gambling deal, was a wedding gift. Louisville's first Chinese restaurant opened soon afterward, joining the small community of Chinese immigrants clustered downtown along Jefferson Street.

The gift from Chin Ming's father, described as a "Chicago property owner," not only provided a method of income but also gave the family an escape from the arcane Chicago Jazz Age underworld. Family history claims that rival gang leader Al Capone assassinated Chin Ming's father in 1937, but the *New York Times* provided a slightly different story. Under the headline "Chinatown Boss Slain in Chicago," the report read, "Chin Jack Lem, 61 years old, one of the wealthiest citizens of Chicago's Chinatown and described as its most feared of the powerful men behind the scenes, was shot and killed tonight as he was walking in the rain in the heart of Chinatown. The assassination was deftly accomplished. The killer, evidently a Chinese, faded away as mysteriously as he appeared."

Removed from the battles between Chicago tongs and possibly Al Capone, Chin Ming became a prospering Louisvillian. According to *The Encyclopedia of Louisville*, his first restaurant, Golden Hour, closed quickly because the staff refused to work in what they believed was a "haunted" building. Chin's

China Inn. *Courtesy of University of Louisville.*

descendants remember Liberty Inn, at the corner of Fourth and Jefferson Streets, as the first of his restaurants—with a large "CHOP SUEY" sign and ornate stained-glass windows on the second floor featuring crossed Chinese and American flags. Whichever history is correct, by the 1940s, Chin Ming was operating three restaurants in the downtown area: Liberty Inn, Loyang Tea Garden at 645 South Fourth and China Inn at 629 South Third.

The World War II era wasn't the easiest time for Chinese people in Louisville, even though many wore badges telling people they weren't Japanese. Chin Ming's son Roosevelt Chin later told the *Courier-Journal* that some of the worst moments came after movie newsreels. "We'd be sitting in the theater and when they showed the Japanese bombing, everybody would hiss," he said. "They'd turn the lights on, we'd all slump in our chairs… People would yell at us, 'You're all the cause of my son being killed.'" Chin Ming fought against this prejudice by forming the American Chinese Committee and continued to work at China Inn until he died there in 1954. His gravestone marks the first Asian American burial in Cave Hill.

In 1960, as more Chinese restaurants (and Chinese people) began to appear in Louisville, Chin Ming's son Richard moved China Inn to South Dixie Highway, renaming it Lotus Restaurant. In 2013, at eighty-one years of age, Richard Chin accepted an award for "Outstanding Deputy of the Year" from the Jefferson County Property Valuation Office. He credited working seven days a week at Louisville's first Chinese restaurants with helping develop his passion for serving the public, which led to his becoming the first Chinese American to hold office in Kentucky as a Republican state senator.

Richard's brother, Roosevelt Chin, left an even greater impression on Louisville. Roosevelt spent his adult life working for Cabbage Patch Settlement House, a charity for at-risk children. A *Courier-Journal* article described Roosevelt, who died in 2007, as "a man whose parents couldn't speak English when they came from China to this country 70 years ago" and who helped children by teaching about "telling the truth, about doing their best and about savoring their worth—no matter what the world seems to assume about them."

To this day, "Cabbage Patch kids" are still inspired by Roosevelt Chin's motto: "You don't work your way out of poverty, you educate your way out." It's an amazing legacy of Louisville's first Chinese community and how far it moved from its early Chicago adventures.

Chapter 14

CANARY COTTAGE

Strange Lands Lead to Shaker Recipes

In an odd setback beside the ornate Palace Theater on Fourth Street, austere columns protect a brick-walled building front, its arched entranceways and rectangular upstairs windows seeming to suggest a design dating from the days of Colonial Williamsburg. That was the intention for this incarnation of R. Menter Wheeler's restaurant empire. Wheeler's awareness that atmosphere could count as much as food and service led to Canary Cottages in multiple cities and the fantastic French Village below the Heyburn Building. It also happened to lead to Shaker lemon pie.

Canary Cottage began as a restaurant in Wheeler's hometown of Winchester, Kentucky, in 1920. Four years later, he opened another in nearby Lexington. In 1928, Wheeler brought the Canary Cottage concept to Louisville. The first design, built inside 621 South Fourth Street, was a replica of an old English inn, complete with exposed overhead beams, a broken flagstone floor, a stone chimney and an open fireplace. The interior had paintings, hangings and furniture designed to re-create the feel of the fifteenth century. Two years later, Wheeler had another inspiration. He leased six thousand square feet in the basement of the Heyburn Building, providing room service to all building offices from a restaurant with decorations imported from France. A 1940s reviewer, Roland L. Hill, described the French Village as having "dining rooms around the side…like the French shops around a public square." He added, "The waitresses are all dressed in French costumes" and assured readers that "the food and service here are like the Canary Cottages."

Canary Cottage in the "old English inn" phase. *Courtesy of University of Louisville.*

A 1936 *Louisville Times* report described the Canary Cottage's offerings as quite extensive, with the luncheon menu alone featuring "thirty-three kinds of sandwiches, a dozen delectable salads and a dozen desserts." Duncan Hines recommended chicken, lamb chops, grilled seafood and spoonbread, but by the time the Bowling Green–based, proto–*Michelin Guide* and future cake mix baron visited the Canary Cottage, the atmosphere had changed again.

Ladies lunching at Canary Cottage. *Courtesy of University of Louisville.*

The *Courier-Journal* effusively reported the Canary Cottage's renovation in 1939: "Just as John D. Rockefeller, Jr. restored from dilapidation Williamsburg, capital and cultural center of the Virginia colony from 1699 to 1779, Louisville contractors united to produce a modern tavern which incorporates the charm of inns of two centuries ago, authentic in detail and faithful in spirit." Expanding next door and pushing the building front back to provide space for square columns, the new Canary Cottage had two entrances: the main door and a separate entrance to the right for the Cocktail Lounge. The lounge was "modern and Continental," while the dining rooms, with fireplaces suggesting colonial Williamsburg, were "antique and American."

Canary Cottage patrons could enjoy "Colonial Dinners" of fried calf brains, "creole spaghetti" with sliced frankfurters, chicken chow mein or country-style fried chicken (which the establishment bragged was "battery fed"). "Kentucky Favorites" included country ham served with spiced crabapple, shoestring potatoes and homemade beaten biscuits.

The French Village closed in 1950. By then, Canary Cottage had expanded to St. Matthews, where it was a fixture for Kentucky dishes such as Hot Browns served in Mary Alice Hadley pottery.

Today, little trace of Wheeler's theme restaurants remains. But it can be argued that the real Kentucky legacy of Canary Cottage and French Village still exists in Shakertown, thanks to Elizabeth Cromwell Kremer. A native of Cynthiana, Kremer had worked in restaurant chains in New York and Cincinnati before coming to Louisville to open the French Village. After successfully managing that launch, she moved back to Cincinnati to manage another Canary Cottage outlet there. (There was also a location in Indianapolis.) Kremer left the restaurant business in 1941, thinking she would never return. But almost thirty years later, she was convinced to come to Shakertown and open a sandwich shop to feed sightseers coming to the restored village. Not satisfied with sandwiches, Kremer painstakingly researched the Shakers and their food, rediscovering such now-classic Kentucky dishes as Shaker lemon pie.

R. Menter Wheeler may have built his Canary Cottage empire out of romantic notions of places from the past. But Elizabeth Kremer gave Kentucky a simple gift that was almost lost forever.

Chapter 15

BLUE BOAR

A "Home-Cooked" Meal with a Side of History and Heritage

For over a century, anyone who stood in line for a school lunch experienced cafeteria-style dining. But pushing a tray along metal tubes while selecting from an array of foods before carrying tray to table was, at one time, quite a novel experience. This semi-self-service style started in New York in the 1880s and spread west, reaching California by 1905. Cafeterias quickly became popular below the Mason-Dixon line. In *Fast Food*, John Jakle and Keith Sculle observed that the mix of "formality and traditionalism" and "solid old-fashioned…cooking" seemed right for southern sensibilities.

Cafeterias needed service on a large scale to be profitable, but profits were to be had. In 1917, A.W.B. Johnson, at the suggestion of a friend in Louisville, took a name from the title of an H.G. Wells novel (*Mr. Britling Sees It Through*) and opened Britling Cafeteria No. 1 in a downtown department store in Birmingham. As the cafeteria idea caught on, Britling cafeterias quickly spread throughout the South and Midwest. An advertisement hailed "the new Britling 'Self-Service' restaurant" as "a distinct innovation, a definite step forward." Pledging "strict adherence to the customs and precedents of home kitchens," Johnson's cafeterias promised "enticing flavors relished by all who still remember the feasts of their childhood." In the late 1920s, Britling came to Louisville, but soon changed its name to one more familiar to Louisvillians: Blue Boar.

Johnson's son, L. Eugene Johnson, opened the first Blue Boar Cafeteria at 644 South Fourth Street in 1931, but by 1936, the original Britling at 410 West Walnut was also being called Blue Boar. Both sites were so busy that

Blue Boar Cafeteria line. *Courtesy of University of Louisville.*

they needed twin serving lines, and both added eating space in basements and balconies. Blue Boar eventually became the name for a cafeteria empire that included Britlings and Blue Boars in various cities, as well as B&W Cafeterias in others.

By 1940, Louisville's demand for stylish steam table dining led Blue Boar to plan a building expansion on Walnut Street. L.E. Johnson told the *Courier-Journal* it would cost "between $75,000 and $100,000" to double capacity to "500 chairs and two steam tables." Two years later, as America was fully engaged in World War II, the $350,000 renovation was unveiled. Another *Courier-Journal* article described the "many historical antiques and authentic Audubon prints in its distinctive interior," along with "a pair of crystal chandeliers from…a mansion outside London." Valued at $1,000 each, the chandeliers "were imported into this country, duty free, in order to preserve them from bombing." They hung over a restaurant whose "color scheme of light blue was suggested by the Apollo Room of the reconstructed Raleigh Tavern at Williamsburg" with "a colorful and historic wallpaper panel" below a curving staircase depicting "a French artist's conception of America in 1834." Rows of mahogany tables sat between walls "papered in a button design much used by Hollywood" and "the last [wallpaper] pattern designed by" James Abbott McNeill Whistler.

One of the proudest people at the 1942 grand reopening of "one of the South's finest cafeterias" was Chef Estel Birkla, who crowed about "the mixers, the ranges, the meat refrigerator, [and] the basement dishwashing equipment." The staff could use all the shiny new tools to turn out the dishes that became Blue Boar classics: iceberg lettuce with cottage cheese dressing, meatloaf with Creole sauce, stuffed pork chops, Salisbury steak, stewed tomatoes, rice Florentine and sugarless apple pie. A secret to Blue Boar's success may have been Chef Birkla's understanding of what the cafeteria had to offer. "The aim is to match home cooking," Birkla said in a 1950 *Courier-Journal* interview. "You're competing with the housewife, not other chefs. If she thinks you cook as well as she does, she'll have the family eat at the restaurant."

In 1955, 410 Walnut was remodeled again. The entire sixty-foot width was replaced with "large plate glass windows with stainless-steel and marble trim." A "power-driven revolving entrance door" was claimed to be the first in the city. In 1959, Blue Boar advertised the chain's coming expansion into Gardiner Lane Shopping Center, "recognizing the growing needs of the Metropolitan Louisville area by providing this new facility for good dining." At the same time, Blue Boar was refusing to recognize the social change happening across the country.

In 1960, the *New York Times* reported that the International Convention of Christian Churches (Disciples of Christ) apologized to its "Negro brethren" for "embarrassing incidents" of racial discrimination during its annual convention, which that year was held in Louisville. Two of the incidents involved Blue Boar, which freely admitted denying service to black people. By the spring of 1961, as civil rights protests gained intensity in Louisville, so did the use of force—particularly at Blue Boar. In *Civil Rights in the Gateway to the South: Louisville, Kentucky, 1945–1980*, Tracy E. K'Meyer wrote:

> *Protest leaders claimed one guard regularly shoved people to the ground and that one young man was "kicked repeatedly." In other incidents guards struck a girl in the breast—she ended up in the hospital—and threw a male student through a plate glass window. Some of the violence took place when cafeteria-employed guards aided the arrest of demonstrators and got overzealous in their use of force. As Gerald White remembered, "They had a paddy wagon at Fourth and Walnut…They would drag you, head bumping, to Fourth Street, in the street, by two legs, to the paddy wagon."*

While demonstrators marched and leaders negotiated, racial tensions increased. Mayor Hoblitzell was antagonistic toward integration, viewing one protest outside Blue Boar and declaring, "This looks like a mob." The students continued their sit-ins until after the 1961 Derby, with establishments like Blue Boar finally relenting because, as demonstrator Gerald White told K'Meyer, "Everybody was losing money."

As the success in civil rights started the hollowing out of Louisville's urban core, Blue Boar continued to expand, opening another location in 1961 at the brand-new Mall St. Matthews, Louisville's first completely enclosed suburban shopping mall. Several years later, Blue Boar continued chasing Louisville's eastern expansion, moving its Shelbyville Road "plant" to the even newer Oxmoor Center. For the flagship downtown Blue Boars, however, things were not so shiny and new.

In 1971, the company closed its cafeteria at 644 South Fourth, which had been in operation for forty years. L.E. Johnson's brother, Wesley, named as general manager, told the *Louisville Times* that he blamed "the decline of the downtown area generally and Fourth Street in particular" for the loss of business. Management expressed hope that customers ("friends, in many cases") would choose Blue Boar's Walnut Street location or "perhaps...one of the five Blue Boar locations [still] scattered around Louisville."

In the 1970s, the company announced it was a "food-service firm" and explored concepts outside the cafeteria model. In 1974, Blue Boar opened its first venture into a table-service operation, called Uncle Sam'z, in a room adjoining the Southland Terrace Shopping Center cafeteria. Calling the concept "food with a view," company officials said to the *Courier-Journal* that they were attempting to "capitalize on the nostalgia wave rolling across the country" by decorating Uncle Sam'z with "Tiffany lights, a loft, booths and 'Coke' chairs." The company also launched a full-service, sit-down restaurant named the Warehouse at the Bashford Manor Mall.

Several years later, Wes Johnson redecorated the Walnut Street Blue Boar, primarily around a new upstairs "Train Room" centered on a large German-manufactured electric train setup. Johnson told the *Louisville Times* that the room, with its "quaint electric train…its wheels clickety-clacking across the rail joints," was one of only several themed rooms in Blue Boar cafeterias featuring items garnered from his "avocation—collecting and buying and selling antiques and other old items." Other themes featured guns, toys, ships, African artifacts and other "old, nostalgia-driven items," which was, unfortunately, what the downtown Blue Boar was becoming.

On August 9, 1979, John Filiatreau broke the news in the *Courier-Journal* that the main downtown Blue Boar would be closing the next day, reminiscing:

It opened for business four months after the attack on Pearl Harbor…It featured a pair of 18th century crystal chandeliers that had been rescued from an English mansion threatened by German bombers…The "Pine Room," to be used for large dinner parties, had the corner cupboards filled with antiques, including Scandinavian pewter, early American candlesticks and china from England and Iran. The menu was varied, the prices low, and the food wholesome and tasty.

Filiatreau noted that, when that Blue Boar opened, the heavyweight boxing champion was Joe Louis, "black people weren't welcome to eat in 'white' restaurants and cafeterias" and the country was "involved in a world war." But by 1979, Walnut Street had "been renamed Muhammad Ali Boulevard in honor of another, entirely different, black boxing champ, a Louisville native who refused to fight in another, entirely different war."

Blue Boar's management again encouraged people to visit the remaining cafeteria locations, most of which were in suburban locations. But most of the Blue Boar cafeterias across the South and Midwest closed by the mid-1990s.

Another Wes Johnson and Blue Boar family descendant became a part of Buckhead Management, Incorporated. In a 2014 interview with *Insider Louisville*'s Steve Coomes, Johnson pushed back against the "negative" concept of "cafeteria food," saying, "In the beginning of it, there was no pre-made anything." Johnson gave credit to the tradition that started with Britling for Buckhead's success, commenting, "Nobody's going to write about our food being cutting edge, but that's OK, because it's not what our customers want." Johnson opened one branch of the firm's Buckhead Mountain Grill in the Gardiner Lane Shopping Center location that once housed a Blue Boar, where perhaps the echoes of those who saw cafeterias as "cutting edge" still remain.

SALISBURY STEAK

Adapted from Blue Boar's recipe published in the *Courier-Journal*. Serves four.

Meat:
½ large onion, peeled and coarsely chopped
about ½ cup bell pepper (red and/or green), seeded and coarsely chopped
2 cloves garlic, quartered

1 pound ground beef
½ teaspoon kosher salt
pinch white pepper
¼ cup cracker meal
1 egg, beaten
2 tablespoons beef broth

Sauce:
generous ½ cup sliced mushrooms
1 tablespoon butter, plus additional if needed
3 scallions (white and green parts), thinly sliced
1½ tablespoons flour
1¼ cups beef broth
salt and pepper to taste

Place onion, bell pepper and garlic in the bowl of a food processor. Pulse until finely chopped.

Mix onion mixture with all remaining meat ingredients in a bowl. Form into four patties. Refrigerate until needed.

Cook mushrooms in a skillet in 1 tablespoon of butter, tossing. After a minute or so, add scallion slices. Continue to toss until done. Set aside.

Preheat oven to 400 degrees.

Cook meat patties in a large skillet, turning once. Remove patties and place in a shallow baking dish.

Reheat the pan drippings in the skillet, adding some butter if needed to create about 2 tablespoons of fat. Sprinkle in flour and whisk until flour is cooked. Pour in beef broth, whisking until smooth and slightly thickened. Add reserved mushrooms and scallions. Season with salt and pepper.

Pour mushroom sauce over patties in baking dish. Heat in oven for 10 minutes.

Chapter 16

STEBBINS

Seafood, Swank and Swizzle

S tebbins Grill opened in 1933 at 412 West Chestnut, promising a place where people "could relax and dine in unhurried comfort and quiet dignity…enjoying the finest of foods, unsurpassed in preparation and service." George Stebbins, who had previously owned a cafeteria, described his restaurant to the *Louisville Times* in 1972 as "an escape from the 'hurly-burly' noise and confusion of the city." It had an eight-foot window displaying "all kinds of fish—red snapper, devil fish, pompano from Miami and even octopus—on cracked ice." For a time, the restaurant was decorated with murals painted by an artist who traded his work for champagne, which Stebbins described as "some of the most beautiful paintings" he'd ever seen. That may have been around the time proto–*Michelin Guide* author Duncan Hines first recommended the restaurant's "stuffed Pompano Louisian" and its lobsters and steaks. The champagne-inspired murals were replaced in the 1940s by "photo-murals" and "translites" featuring Kentucky scenes of Derbies, rail and river transportation and shout-outs to the tobacco industry.

Steak and seafood were the restaurant's big sellers. Stebbins said that "big platters of jumbo shrimp," with sinus-searing, horseradish-laced cocktail sauce, "went over best with Louisvillians." The locals didn't want anything fancy. (Stebbins recalled, "People in those days didn't think much of olive oil.") But they did want hickory plank–broiled steak and fish and "garlic toast," two things Stebbins claimed as his "innovations." Stebbins's customers liked the way the hickory planks added flavor and "absorbed the fat," which may not have been missed with the usual "french fried onion

Above: Stebbins Grill. *Courtesy of University of Louisville.*

Right: Swizzle, 1951. *Courtesy of University of Louisville.*

rings" accompanying them. In 1954, the *Louisville Times* raved, "For sea food dinners par excellence, fine steaks, cocktails supreme, and efficient service in a pleasant atmosphere…you can't beat Stebbin's Grill."

Another of Stebbins's "innovations" came when he opened a second steak place across the street at 421 West Chestnut in 1945. That restaurant, the Swizzle, was later called Stebbins Steak House and is now the site of the Body Shop Lounge, where the old neon sign has been altered to advertise "Girls Girls Girls." In addition to meat and seafood, "long sticks" with "three feet at the bottom" mixed a patron's drink "just by swirling it." (It is possible this particular innovation came to Stebbins after a trip to the Caribbean, where swizzle stick bushes grow in the wild.)

In the late 1950s, Stebbins turned his eponymous restaurant over to another owner (Leo Weil of Leo's Hideway), who turned the "swanky seafood" restaurant into Leo's Twinburger. Stebbins retired in 1965. And though he said in 1972 that he missed "the fun and hard work of running a restaurant," Stebbins's steak and seafood establishments have vanished from Louisville. Swizzle sticks, however, may still be found in many bars around town—including the hip cocktail lounge Meta just down from where Stebbins's Swizzle used to be.

Chapter 17

KAELIN'S

Bootlegger to "Birthplace" of the Cheeseburger

Carl Kaelin was a man who knew how to take advantage. When a telephone operator's voice intrigued him, he convinced a friend working for the phone company to introduce him to the woman he would marry. A trained mechanic who couldn't find work during the Depression, Carl turned to bootlegging, aided by his new wife, Margaret. Their daughter, Irma Raque, recalled in a 1992 *Chicago Tribune* interview that her mother "sewed a bunch of pockets on the inside of a coat" and her father "would load those pockets with whiskey and make the rounds of his customers with Mom's tailoring discreetly hiding his merchandise." As Prohibition ended, Carl decided to try his hand at chicken farming in Fern Creek. As a city boy, it wasn't his calling. But one day in 1934, when cleaning out some old newspapers lining the coops, Carl saw a real estate ad for a tavern on Newburg Road. Carl saw an opportunity and, though he had no experience with food or government-licensed alcohol sales, bought the business.

In the early days, Carl managed the downstairs while Margaret cooked orders upstairs in the family apartment's tiny kitchen. "Daddy would sit me at the top of the steps," Raque recalled to *Food & Dining Magazine*. "When he got an order, he would call up and say: 'Tell your mother to send down a ham on rye.'" Despite the awkward kitchen arrangements, the Kaelins attracted the attention of the principal of St. Agnes Elementary School, located directly across the street. The principal proposed paying to provide the kids' lunches, and the Kaelins agreed. This led to Margaret preparing

Kaelin's and St. Agnes School. *Courtesy of University of Louisville.*

quite a lot of cheese sandwiches, which led to the world's (or at the very least, Kentucky's) very first cheeseburger.

The way the Kaelins tell it, everything started with some American cheese left over from the schoolchildren's lunches. Margaret was cooking some hamburgers for a hungry Carl while wrapping up the cheese. Margaret told the *Courier-Journal* that, as she turned the hamburgers, Carl said, "'Lay a piece of cheese on that hamburger and let it melt'— and I did and he liked it. And then I made him the third one and then I said, 'Well, I believe I'll try one if they're that good.' And I liked them, too." The Kaelins then tested their melted cheese–topped burger on a few regulars. The men thought the new item would be a hit, and as Raque recalled, "One of the guys, 'Broad' Willinger, whose name indicates how much he loved to eat, said 'Why not call it Kaelin's Cheeseburger?'" They did, and it quickly became a hit.

The Kaelins were soon going through almost four hundred pounds of hamburger every weekend, with most of the patties covered with cheese. During World War II, servicemen on leave from Fort Knox discovered the tavern with its "Cheeseburgers" sign and supposedly spread the word about cheeseburgers to every corner of America—that is, unless the soldiers were from Pasadena, California. Or Los Angeles. Or Denver. Or Bloomington-Normal, Illinois. Because while the restaurant at the corner of Newburg and Speed became known by mayoral decree as the "birthplace of the cheeseburger," other places had come up with the idea of placing a slice of cheese on an almost-cooked burger, some even earlier than the Kaelins.

Hamburgers had appeared in America by the late 1800s and quickly became quite popular. A 1928 menu for O'Dell's in Los Angeles offered a "cheeseburger on a bun" for fifteen cents—the same price of Kaelin's "original" cheeseburger. The proprietor of Denver's Humpty-Dumpty Drive-in sued for trademark protection of the word "cheeseburger" in 1935. And the "Memphis Cheeseburger Trial" of 1938 pitted W.W. Stevens of Dallas against the Toddle House chain, whose defense was based in part on reports of an Illinois restaurant making Limburger cheese–topped burgers as early as 1913. This daunting evidence that the cheeseburger was not invented in Louisville was perhaps unknown to the Kaelins, who (like everyone else in those days) lacked access to the Internet and may very well have never been west of the Mississippi.

Original idea or not, the cheeseburgers at Kaelin's were a hit, and the restaurant even initiated curb service early in the postwar era. In the 1950s, Kaelin's was a popular hangout for many, including a man who would go on to fame with another invention—Kentucky Fried Chicken. Harland Sanders was a good friend of Carl Kaelin's and always ate cheeseburgers when he came by the restaurant. In the mid-1950s, as Sanders explored his vision of pressure-fried, proprietarily spiced chicken, Kaelin switched his own fried chicken for that of the man who would become the "Colonel." However, when Sanders offered Kaelin a chicken franchise, according to the *Highland Herald*, Carl "couldn't see putting 10,000 bucks into it" and declined.

A *Louisville Times* reviewer encapsulated Kaelin's in 1975 as a place where people could "dine fairly inexpensively in a homey atmosphere with very informal service," adding, "You're not likely to shout any huzzahs about the food, but it won't give you heartburn either." In front of the restaurant was a sign requesting: "If you can't stop, please wave." It was an idea that came to Carl after seeing a similar sign on a trip to Florida, and it became something the restaurant was known for almost as much as its burgers.

Carl Kaelin died in 1978, having risen from bootlegging mechanic to president of the Louisville Restaurant Association, honored throughout America (except for a few surly folk in places like California and Colorado) as the inventor of the cheeseburger. Irma Raque and other Kaelin family members continued to operate the restaurant until 2004. Other restaurateurs attempted to open coffee shops and Irish-themed eateries on the site, but now the former Kaelin's sits vacant, the "Cheeseburger" sign pushed to the side. Today, the Kaelin family knows they may not have

Chapter 18

HASENOUR'S

Turning Friendship into a Legend

E d Hasenour was more than a host. For years, he was the face of his namesake restaurant—appearing seemingly everywhere during service, offering advice in the newspapers and sponsoring countless civic activities. Earl Cox, one of Louisville's legendary sportswriters, said, "Most restaurants have patrons. Hasenour's Restaurant under the ownership of Ed Hasenour had friends."

Hasenour started his first restaurant in 1934, after dust aggravated his asthma when he worked at a flour mill. He and a partner opened a cafeteria at Floyd and Breckinridge Streets, just behind Male High School, serving simple foods like roast beef sandwiches. Despite being open from 6:00 a.m. to midnight the first day, the pair took in less than $10. Soon, the partner became discouraged, and Hasenour borrowed $225 and bought him out, determined to make the business succeed. One early strategy Hasenour hit on was simple kindness. Male sports coaches had been bringing the athletes over to eat before games. At the height of the Depression, a lot of Male's athletes didn't have money, but as Earl Cox remembered, "Ed saw to it that none of the Purples went hungry." The charity didn't immediately help Hasenour's bottom line. He recalled in a 1984 interview a time when "a driver delivered two cases of Cokes," and Hasenour had to tell him, "I didn't have the money, could he come back after lunch?" (According to Hasenour, the answer was "no.")

The 1937 flood broke out the windows and swamped the steam tables of Hasenour's cafeteria, but the damage was quickly repaired, and a new flood of carpenters, painters and plumbers streamed in. Hasenour's wife,

Marcy, oversaw the steam tables as factory workers, deliverymen and others came in for a quick meal and a glass of beer. Ed managed the cash register and customer relations, along with the cafeteria's pinball machines, which baseball Hall of Famer Pee Wee Reese remembered to the *Courier-Journal* as a profit-making enterprise that "probably paid everything off." Prior to becoming Jackie Robinson's teammate and main defender as he desegregated baseball, Reese would sip beer and "dump nickels into the machine." Then World War II arrived, and Hasenour's became busy with defense plant workers while continuing to build relationships with athletes, sponsoring a high school baseball team.

When the war ended, the defense workers began to find other jobs, and Ed Hasenour began to imagine a life beyond the cafeteria. In 1952, he bought the existing liquor license and arranged for a lease on a property at the corner of Barret Avenue and Oak Street. He hired a bartender, a waiter and a few cooks and opened what he called a "tablecloth restaurant" to complement his cafeteria trade. Hasenour said he later found out that friends in the business thought he would soon be bankrupt, as the former "restaurant" he had taken over was actually a gambling front that nobody thought could actually work as a food service business. But Ed Hasenour was not afraid of a challenge.

A 1952 grand opening ad for Hasenour's Dining & Cocktail Lounge promoted a restaurant open from 9:00 a.m. to 1:00 a.m serving "short orders, fine steaks [and] choice sandwiches," along with "fine whiskies" and "de luxe service." The student athletes Hasenour had fed through the Depression and World War II were growing prosperous, and Hasenour's grew along with them. While people in overalls were still welcome in his cafeteria, their presence uptown "got to be a problem." Hasenour told the *Courier-Journal* that "higher prices straightened that out," however, as dinners went from $2.00 up to $2.50 for the lobster tail, which was "a little steep for a working man."

As his restaurants continued to become more successful, Ed Hasenour did not slow down. He would set an alarm not long after the uptown restaurant closed to make sure the baker who worked behind his cafeteria would be at work on time. Affable and deeply interested in customer relations, Hasenour was a perfectionist behind the scenes. His daughter, Marcia, wrote that her father "was a hard-working German who believed there was only one way to do things—the right way," adding that "when the waitresses say, 'Beware, here HE comes,' they meant Dad was unhappy about something and was fussing. Dad's biggest pet peeve was having dirty tables sitting unoccupied

Hasenour's bar. *Courtesy of John Nation.*

while his customers were waiting…He said he wasn't making any money when people were waiting for tables."

Hasenour worked hard at not only the restaurant business but also its promotion. He continued to sponsor sporting events and athletes. The restaurant drew local bigwigs and early local TV celebrities. Marcia Hasenour remembers seeing *T-Bar-V Ranch Time*'s Randy Atcher and Tom "Cactus" Brooks, "Uncle" Ed Kallay and many others. Ed Hasenour was not afraid to literally get his face out in print. Although the restaurant primarily relied on word-of-mouth advertising, regular "Food for Thought" advertorials featured Ed Hasenour's photo along with small recipes and tips, always leading to the "thought" that a meal at Hasenour's Restaurant would be an excellent idea.

The 1960s brought some problems to Hasenour's. In 1964, the restaurant was the scene of a "stand-in" protest in which eleven demonstrators were arrested. Asked about it years later, Hasenour told the *Courier-Journal*, "At that point in time, our trade wasn't ready for this integration business." Hasenour said he locked the restaurant's doors when demonstrators arrived because he "looked at them and saw it was the easiest way to avoid trouble." But not long thereafter, a black minister went to Hasenour's for lunch with a white colleague and was served. In 1965, the restaurant had its liquor license suspended for ten days after officials found pinball machines at the place were paying off to customers. (There is no word on whether Pee Wee Reese was nearby sipping a beer.)

The 1970s went a bit better. Hasenour closed the cafeteria, concentrating his family's efforts on the Barret and Oak establishment. He helped form the Kentucky Restaurant Association, became president of the Greater Louisville Convention Bureau and was named "Restaurateur of the Year." A 1972 guide said that Hasenour's provided "consistently good food and attentive service in a comfortable atmosphere" and recommended "Oysters Bienville (topped with a spicy minced-seafood sauce)" and "Kentucky Country Ham and Red Eye Gravy (not overly salty)" as well as "Derby Pie" (evidently not yet trademarked).

If there was one thing Ed Hasenour loved as much as his restaurant, it was the Kentucky Derby. Special menus through the years featured Derby winners, and Hasenour continued the track visits he'd begun as a young man—though he graduated from paying a quarter "to climb a fence and jump down" into the Downs to parading his family through the exclusive clubhouse area. Hasenour's Derby Brunch buffet featured "country ham, fried chicken, chicken ala king, biscuits, grits, asparagus, hash brown potatoes, mini desserts and more," drawing people such as St. Louis baseball great Stan Musial, trumpeter Al Hirt and sportscaster Howard Cosell. Hasenour was also behind the "Run for the Rosé" and the Derby Festival Balloon Race. In 1980, he was presented with a picture of the first Balloon Race in Iroquois Park inscribed with the statement: "Ed Hasenour—the skies of Louisville bloom each spring because of you."

In 1979, Hasenour's added the Atrium, increasing the restaurant's seating capacity to 350. The adjoining arched brick area with ferns and hanging yarn sculptures was described by the *New York Times* as "an elegant addition…that has its own décor, its own chef and its own menu of Continental dishes." While Hasenour's had sauerbraten, Delmonico steak and shrimp cocktail, the Atrium offered "Sole Paupiette, Frog Legs Provencale, or Escargots Bouchee." The restaurants advertised themselves as "Louisville's freshest tradition."

In 1984, Hasenour's celebrated its fiftieth anniversary. Supposedly semi-retired, Hasenour was still spending six to eight hours a day around the restaurant making sure "the place is clean…the service is good and… the regulars [aren't] playing liar's poker around the bar in the middle of the afternoon." Hasenour told a reporter, "I've worked all my life, I

Mr. Hasenour with his wife and daughter. *Courtesy of John Nation.*

didn't play golf or anything, and when you're like that the best thing you can do is work."

In 1987, Ed Hasenour was diagnosed with cancer, which spread rapidly. Though he was getting weaker, his daughter wrote that he "had to make sure his business was still there and everything was running properly" despite the fact that "Mother had given me instructions NOT to stop at the restaurant." Marcia Hasenour recalled her father saying that he "was going to die anyhow, so he might as well do what he wanted." He died in early 1988.

Hasenour's son, Lee, who had come up with the idea for the Atrium, continued to run the restaurants and tried to change with the times. In 1989, the *Courier-Journal* reported that Lee Hasenour wanted "to encourage the development of a regional cuisine from classic Kentucky favorites, such as country ham and lamb" with a menu featuring "recipes that are more palatable to today's calorie-conscious consumers but still please traditionalists who love Southern cooking." But while Hasenour's still hosted proms and wedding parties, the business never recovered from the passing of its founder. After tax liabilities and attempts to reorganize, Hasenour's closed its doors for good in 1996, and the restaurant's property was auctioned off.

In 1988, both chambers of the state legislature passed resolutions honoring "a great Kentuckian, Ed Hasenour" who operated "one of the best known restaurants in Louisville." The resolutions quoted Hasenour as saying "the three secrets to his success were quality food, quality service and cleanliness." Hasenour may never have gotten the hang of cooking, but he became "a master at meeting, greeting and making friends."

Sauerbraten

Adapted from *Hasenour's: The History of a Louisville Restaurant Tradition.*
Serves six to eight.

Marcia Hasenour's book provided a "restaurant-sized recipe," calling for fifty pounds of beef and one and a half gallons of vinegar. This is a more manageable version.

Marinade:
2 cups cold water
2 cups red wine vinegar
1 onion, peeled and sliced
2 carrots, peeled and roughly chopped
2 stalks celery, roughly chopped
4 tablespoons brown sugar
4 cloves garlic, peeled and halved
2 teaspoons kosher salt
2 bay leaves
1 teaspoon black peppercorns
1 small lemon, sliced
1 teaspoon dried thyme

3- or 4-pound bottom round or eye of round roast
4 to 6 tablespoons fat (neutral oil, bacon drippings and/or butter), divided
1 cup red wine
3 or 4 tablespoons flour
10 gingersnap cookies, crushed
ground black pepper

Mix together all marinade ingredients in a large pot or bowl. Add meat. Cover and refrigerate 3 days, turning meat occasionally.

Remove meat from marinade and dry off with paper towels, reserving marinade.

Heat about a tablespoon of fat in a large pot or Dutch oven. Brown meat well on all sides, adding another tablespoon of fat if needed. Pour marinade and wine over and bring to a boil. Reduce heat and cover. Braise at a low simmer (turning meat occasionally) until meat is tender, about 2 to 3 hours.

Remove meat from pot and place on a large platter or cutting board, tenting with aluminum foil.

Strain solids from marinade, reserving the liquid. Skim and discard fat that rises to the top.

In a large saucepan, melt 3 to 4 tablespoons of fat. Add an equal amount of flour, whisking to make a roux. Slowly add reserved marinade liquid, whisking constantly until incorporated. Simmer for a few minutes, stirring, until slightly thickened. Stir in crushed cookies. Stir until smooth. Season well with pepper.

Slice meat. Serve with sauce and potato pancakes.

Chapter 19

LUVISI'S

From Italian Novelty to Louisville Institution

For a while, at least, it seems Ernest Luvisi served pizza. A photograph of his restaurant at 448 South Fifth Street, taken sometime after World War II, shows a neon "PIZZA" sign hanging above an older marquee for Luvisi Restaurant, its triangular front flanked by more neon advertising "SPAGHETTI," "ITALIAN DINNERS," "CHICKEN" and "STEAKS—CHOPS."

Ernest Luvisi claimed Louisville's first pizza was baked in his restaurant during World War II, at a party some fifty to sixty East Coast Italian American soldiers threw from 2:00 to 4:00 a.m. Luvisi's story was backed up in 1957 by the Louisville Restaurant Association. But Luvisi's son, Lee, whose fame as a classical pianist eclipsed his father's as a restaurateur, has his doubts. "He always said he cooked the first pizza," Lee Luvisi says, but added, "My father, with all due respect, loved to pop off about sorts of things." Lee Luvisi does remember, "as a kid, during the Second World War…seeing the place packed with soldiers," the lines of pass-holding GIs from Fort Knox extending "outside the front door, all the way around to the corner." Whether serving pizza or not, the popularity of Luvisi's extended well into the late 1950s. But its real legacy lives on in Louisville's cultural heritage.

Lee Luvisi doesn't know exactly when his father opened his eatery in Louisville, but one of the earliest menus still in his possession dates from somewhere in the 1930s. It is titled "Luvisi Italian Restaurant." Given the long tradition of Italian saloon owners, Louisville was not unfamiliar with

Luvisi's, "The Spaghetti Specialist." *Courtesy of University of Louisville.*

Italians—but the menu suggests the city's residents were slightly suspicious. A boxed-in "assurance to our patrons" proclaimed that "the Spaghetti" as well as meats and other ingredients were "the very finest obtainable." The menu focused on Italian dishes such as "Spaghetti with Meat Ball," minestrone and mostaccioli. It offered a special "Chicken A La Cacciatora," explained as "Chicken baked in Italian Mushroom Sauce," served with potatoes, choice of salad and coffee, tea or milk, for seventy-five cents. There was also an assortment of antipasti, such as salami, sardines and anchovies; a "special Italian salad"; and spumoni ice cream. But, being Louisville, there was also steak.

At the time of the 1939 Derby, the restaurant was still known as "Luvisi Italian." Ernest's son, Lee, was only two, and as Louisville became more familiar with the Luvisi family, American-style entrées began to get equal billing with Italian fare. Spaghetti, ravioli and mostaccioli were still front and center, but "Chicken Ala Cacciatora" (then accompanied by "French Fried Potatoes, Spaghetti") shared space with two steaks, fried chicken and pork chops—though they came with a side of spaghetti.

The Derby still gets notice from local restaurants, but the races held special attention for Ernest Luvisi—and are perhaps one reason his son

Luvisi's interior. *Courtesy of Lee Luvisi.*

became the classical music legend he is today. Lee Luvisi describes his father as "an avid horse race fan. He went out to Churchill Downs every day of his adult life, every meet." Lee remembers that, one particular day, around 1945, "My father put all the money he'd won that day onto the longest shot available. The horse won. He could have bought me a violin, he could have bought me a flute or a saxophone, but he bought me a piano. So I'm a pianist." Lee Luvisi, of course, isn't simply "a pianist." A student of Rudolf Serkin and Mieczyslaw Horszowski, he gained early fame, touring nationally and internationally to great acclaim. But he chose to return home in 1963, becoming artist in residence at the University of Louisville School of Music while remaining active in chamber societies and giving occasional solo performances. Today, he still gives "one or two recitals a year." Lee Luvisi recalls that, when he toured across the country, he was amazed at how many people "in some place like Nebraska or Maine would come up and say, 'Oh, I ate in your father's restaurant when I was in Fort Knox.'"

Lee believes one reason for Luvisi's popularity was the presence of his father, who "welcomed everybody that walked into the restaurant and glad-handed them." The elder Luvisi became involved with numerous civic organizations. As Ernest became more of a presence on the Louisville business scene, his son became identified as a piano prodigy. Lee Luvisi never played at his father's restaurant, which had no live entertainment—unless his father "decided to start singing." Lee recalls, "My father was a very gregarious person, sometimes to my embarrassment…He loved people, and he loved to sing. He would take any opportunity in the restaurant with anybody who walked in with an instrument to start singing with them." Lee Luvisi says his father's love of music and performance helped develop his own interest, but this wasn't always a blessing. He remembers, "When my parents would travel, they always liked to go to fancy restaurants or sometimes a nightclub, and they'd drag me along, which was not always appropriate. Even less appropriate were the times my father would have a little bit too much to drink, and he couldn't resist going up on stage, to the microphone, and say, 'My son here is going to play something!'"

Ernest Luvisi's rising stature also seemed to make his menu even more Americanized. A 1948 menu features racing horses on its cover, and the restaurant's $1.75 "Italian Dinner" shared space with shrimp cocktail, sliced chicken, baked ham and soft drinks. The facing panel offered steaks, fish, chicken, country ham, frog legs and other dishes, the only Italian entrée being "Veal Scaloppine, a la Toscana." "Chicken Ala Cacciatora" was no more, and the spaghetti side dish had been replaced by hash browns.

This mainstreaming of what had been an Italian-centered service did not stop Luvisi's popularity. The "Spaghetti Specialist" had shifted focus to filet mignon and mushroom sauce, broiled lobster tails and "French Fried

Luvisi's menu, 1948. *Courtesy of Lee Luvisi.*

Ernest Luvisi shaking hands with Liberace. *Courtesy of Lee Luvisi.*

Shrimp," but the swells kept coming in. "My father had all kinds of celebrities that came into the restaurant when they were in Louisville," says Lee Luvisi, who provided a picture of his father with Liberace, who "stood for everything I don't stand for as a classical artist." Lee also remembers the restaurant being popular with the clergy from the Cathedral of the Assumption across the street. "I remember all the priests used to come over to the restaurant," Luvisi says. "They knew how to party, let me tell you."

Ernest Luvisi closed his restaurant before 1960. The building that once may have hosted Louisville's first pizza party was torn down, later to be replaced by the peacefully landscaped lot known as Founders Square. Pizza is available just about everywhere one looks in Louisville, and ravioli and spumoni are also no longer foreign concepts. There may no longer be a Luvisi singing on Fifth Street, but Lee Luvisi thinks his dad would be "happy that people are remembering his restaurant." Ernest Luvisi would undoubtedly also be happy that, because of his son's talent, the music of a Luvisi is still heard in Louisville.

Chapter 20
KUPIE'S

Copyright-Skirting Cuteness Across from the Cathedral

Rose Cecil O'Neill unveiled the first Kewpie in 1909. O'Neill was already a nationally known illustrator whose work appeared in *Ladies' Home Journal, Good Housekeeping* and the humor magazine *Puck*. O'Neill's Kewpies were elf-like infants with topknots and big smiles. O'Neill described them as "a sort of little round fairy whose one idea is to teach people to be merry and kind at the same time" and dreamt up the name because it reminded her of "Cupid." The cherubic Kewpies were an immediate hit around the world. "You get a Kewpie doll" became a catchphrase for bestowing a modest prize, and the cherubic figures started selling Japanese mayonnaise as early as 1925. By the eve of World War II, there were many nods to the now-iconic doll. One of them was Kupie, a lunch place that opened near the corner of Fifth and Walnut Streets around 1940. According to Laura Leong, one of the owners of Hoe Kow Restaurant, before Kupie arrived, her family operated a laundry and lived at 456 South Fifth Street until they were "evicted" around 1939. Moving in was Daynon Hicks, who may have had some knowledge of Cupid himself.

Hicks's Kupie Lunch advertised itself as "a good place to eat" with "excellent coffee and sandwiches." The signs, plates and matchbooks for the restaurant featured several iterations of almost-Kewpies—some in pants and sweaters on skis, others wearing only chef's hats and butt-baring aprons. It is not known whether Kupie's waitstaff wore the same sort of outfits. But one can deduce that, at Kupie's for a time, there was a bit of love in the air.

Kupie Lunch. *Courtesy of University of Louisville.*

Daynon Hicks's restaurant was probably doing fairly good business by the late 1940s, although Erma Dick, who was about to establish the Old House, must not have had a very good opinion of it. In her autobiography, Dick described that block as "filled with bookies and joints," the only exceptions being "Luvisi's fine Italian restaurant and Jerry Rosenberg's impressive liquor store." Whether or not Kupie's was a "joint" remains in dispute, but what is certain is that previously married Daynon had become quite taken with a young waitress, Mary, who had worked there for several years before becoming the second Mrs. Hicks in 1947.

Two weeks after they were married, Daynon Hicks opened Hick's Drive-In in Shively, leaving Mary to manage the air-conditioned Kupie Lunch, which was by then offering its steaks and chops for breakfast, lunch and dinner. She managed the restaurant for three years, but in 1950, things changed. Daynon's first wife died, and he brought his two daughters to live with him and Mary. As set forth in a published legal opinion, what happened next was "the presence of the two children in the home contributed to the domestic strife between the parties since they, apparently, failed to adjust well to the changed conditions of their home." Daynon Hicks sold Kupie in 1950. Mary moved out and filed for divorce in 1952.

Daynon continued to operate his Shively restaurant for several more years. It is unclear what happened to Mary, but the site of the original Kupie Lunch was, along with Luvisi's, knocked down and replaced by Founders Square.

The Kupie name survived in Louisville for a long time afterward. Kupie Restaurant and Lounge, on Chestnut near Fifth Street, became a convenient hangout for many media personalities. With a lounge and restaurant separated by a thin wall and a ceiling stained brown from cigarette smoke, Kupie's was the place to get an egg-and-cheese sandwich, a drink or some gossip at virtually any hour of the day. In the 1970s, legendary WAKY disc jockey Bill Bailey had to apologize for an on-air retelling of a joke that he heard from a doctor at Kupie's involving ethnic slurs against both Polish and Vietnamese people. Bailey supposedly said, "People are too damned sensitive. It's just a matter of trying to have a good time." Not as good of a time as Daynon Hicks may have had around the corner, but the sign of the Cupid (or Kewpie or Kupie) stood at that spot until it, too, was razed in the late 1990s.

Chapter 21

THE PLANTATION

An Elaborate, Embarrassing Way to Symbolize a City

The Seelbach was originally lauded as Louisville's "first European hotel." With the opening of the Seelbach's doors in 1905, its lavish furnishings and grand spaces drew great acclaim. But by the eve of World War II, the Seelbach had changed owners, faced increasing competition and was showing its age. The Eppley Hotels Company of Omaha, which had owned the Seelbach since 1929, debuted a new place for "bending a convivial elbow, eating and dancing" in a space that had previously been rented out as a drugstore. Called the Plantation, the club's main feature was a twenty-five-foot-wide diorama, described as "a combination model and picture having perspective and depth."

Established in 1917, Eppley eventually grew to own twenty-two properties and was one of the earliest hotel chains. Many of its hotels featured public rooms with themes specific to their locations, a way to differentiate themselves through ornamentation while connecting the company to local interests. In an Iowa hotel, Eppley commissioned Grant Wood, painter of the iconic *American Gothic*, to create a mural for the "Corn Room." Conical piles of harvested corn are the central theme of this work, which now hangs in a museum in Sioux City. It's a quiet, contemplative and inspirational piece of art—a far cry from the ornate, awful intricacy of the Plantation diorama.

A 1941 *Courier-Journal* article cited the "noted" Gus A. Renze Company of Omaha, which made "floats for the Mardi Gras and whose work…[was] shown in every exposition in the United States since 1895," as the creator

Plantation at the Seelbach. *Courtesy of University of Louisville.*

of the Plantation's diorama, described as depicting "an old Kentucky plantation with lights and animation synchronized and operating on schedule time."

> *The manor house and the slave quarters are in the foreground; in the background is the river. At intervals a Negro under a tree lifts his jug and takes a drink; Mandy does her washing moving slowly and two pickaninnies dance and play the banjo.*
>
> *On the porch of the big house a beautifully gowned woman moves forward at intervals. The light changes and there is a stunning glow followed by darkness. Lights from the town across the river are reflected in the water and a steamboat comes round the bend as a mournful blast from its horn is heard.*

The "temporarily" distracting diorama wasn't the only attraction of the Plantation. Additional features included "silhouettes of plantation life in gold and vermillion" and a large dance floor. Peggy Fuller, "the girl with a thousand tunes," often opened the cocktail hour. The "sensational" Plantation served a dinner of "four full courses 95¢ up" starting at 5:30 p.m. A sign out front advertised "2 shows nitely" and no cover charge.

Chapter 22

LEO'S HIDEAWAY

A Bet Begins a Louisville Aristocrat

Leo Weil was the first to arrive in the morning and the last to leave at night at the Fulton Fish Market, even while he was running the wholesaler along with four retail fish markets, a fish brokerage concern, three restaurants, a catering service and real estate, not to mention his financial backing of other Louisville fish markets and restaurants. Weil was known as the "Seafood King," and his restaurant, Leo's Hideaway, by 1959 had surpassed Stebbins Grill as the place in Louisville for "those who recognize[d] the gastronomic value of choice seafood."

Weil had taken over the former Stebbins Grill, transforming it into teen-centric Leo's Twinburger, while saying the demand for "swanky seafood dinners had shifted." Shifted, that is, to Leo's Hideaway, down an alley at 115 West Jefferson—a restaurant Weil had opened in 1942 on a bet. In a *Courier-Journal* interview, Weil explained the bet:

> *Over some drinks at Stebbins' one night, I was bragging that I could open a restaurant even in an alley and in three months be selling more fish than Stebbins was selling. A Stebbins partner bet $300 I couldn't do it. I owned an old, unused building at 115 W. Jefferson, near the Haymarket, and he agreed that the dilapidated garage in back of the building could be considered an alley location. Meat rationing was on when I opened Leo's Hideaway in that garage. Steaks were hard to get. I started advertising in newspapers that "Leo Has Steaks—Delicious Mouth-Watering Halibut Steaks, Salmon Steaks, Swordfish Steaks."*

Leo's Hideway postcard. *Courtesy of University of Kentucky.*

That newspaper advertising did the trick. I collected the bet in one month.

Weil not only won the bet but also continued to grow the Hideaway's business. In a 1954 "Dining Out" guide, the *Louisville Times* described Leo's Hideaway as "the aristocrat of seafood restaurants." The "dilapidated garage" had become a three-story restaurant, serving "Leo's special deviled crab, in shell," "genuine fillet of sole," "Alaskan chicken halibut," several varieties of lobster (Maine, South African, Thermidor and "dainties") and a selection of fish from Norwegian waters.

It seems Weil was the first American distributor of Icelandic cod, which became a Friday fried fish staple for Louisville's heavy population of Catholics and possibly earned Weil the nickname of "Cod Father." At the very least, it earned him the admiration of Icelanders, who awarded Weil their highest civilian honor, "The Order of The Falcon," for his success in importing their fish to America.

Weil also gained the admiration of *Courier-Journal* owner Barry Bingham Sr., who had been tasked by the mayor with helping integrate Louisville's restaurants. According to *The Patriarch*, Bingham's first success was the "popular seafood restaurant called Leo's Hideaway, where the proprietor initially integrated the dining room by inviting two black ministers to dinner." Several of the white patrons took offense but calmed down when Weil pointed out they were men of the cloth. Bingham related, however, that, as the customers sat back down, "one of the black men pulled out a racing form," adding, "I wish that had not happened." The restaurant was desegregated, and Leo's Hideaway led the rest of Louisville's restaurant community into integration.

Weil died in 1977. Leo's Hideaway has been replaced by a parking garage, part of the urban renewal that razed so much of the old downtown core. But every time a Louisvillian bites into a codfish sandwich, he can thank the "Seafood King" whose restaurant once reigned over Jefferson Street.

Chapter 23

THE OLD HOUSE

Intriguing History Meets Irascible, Independent Woman

Erma Biesel Dick operated the Old House from 1946 until 1979. Mrs. Dick was raised in Indiana and, according to her autobiography, "barely managed to graduate from Jeffersonville High School in 1927." After less than a year at Spencerian Business College, she went to work for Lewis Kaye, manager of a branch of Citizens Fidelity National Bank. Kaye left the bank and became a partner at the W.L. Lyons brokerage firm, taking Mrs. Dick (then married to her first husband, Edward Biesel) with him as his secretary.

When World War II broke out, Kaye enlisted as a naval aviator, granting Mrs. Dick "general power of attorney" to take care of his business while he served aboard an aircraft carrier. As a manager, and "being on an expense account," Mrs. Dick traveled to New York and New Orleans on behalf of her boss, often going "to the most famous and finest of the restaurants" in those cities, spending hours talking to owners and managers and always leaving with menus, which would appear later as decorations in her own restaurant. While Mrs. Dick had assisted her German grandmother in a farmhouse kitchen, her real education in cuisine came from her business trips. She said, "The more I learned, the more I yearned to have a restaurant like those I visited."

While Kaye was at war, on his behalf, Mrs. Dick purchased six adjoining old buildings in the 400 block of Fifth Street, which she claimed was at the time "filled with bookies and joints." The block had once been residential, but over time, storefronts had been added and the buildings became businesses, with one exception: the townhouse at 432 South Fifth. Built around 1829 in the late Federal style, the three-story brick house is one of the only examples of an antebellum townhome remaining in Louisville's downtown. Because of a fireplace mantel nearly identical to the one in Federal Hill near Bardstown (the former plantation now known as "My Old Kentucky Home" because it inspired Stephen Foster to write the state's official song), it was long rumored the house once belonged to John Rowan. This theory has largely been discredited, but all agree that it became the home of generations of medical professionals, including William McDowell, known for his study of tuberculosis, and three generations of dentists named Canine. The dental offices were a place of invention. The Canines were granted a patent for using celluloid in the making of dental plates. Dr. J.F. Canine, who made dental instruments on the premises, was one of the first in the South to use a steam-powered drill. The Canines also were the first in Louisville to heat their home with steam and wrapped their own dynamos to create the city's first electrically lit home. (The bright lights so startled the neighbors that they called the fire department, believing the building was ablaze.)

Mrs. Dick created a steady income stream from the rental of the former Canine home at 432, as she had with the other 400 block properties and with Kaye's other interests. When Kaye returned from the war, he found his affairs in such good order that he told Mrs. Dick he would never be able to repay her. She responded by telling him of her ambition to go into the restaurant business, adding, "I will work with you, but I will no longer work *for* you."

Erma Dick's autobiography detailed the challenges of opening her first restaurant, including persuading an "aged and unworldly" priest at the Cathedral of the Assumption across the street to grant a waiver of the two-hundred-foot limit for liquor sales near a church. Using her then-seven-year-old son as a guarantor of innocence, Mrs. Dick obtained her waiver and set about renovating the old Canine home into a restaurant. She cut out the Canines' coal-fired steam boiler with an acetylene torch, leaving the floor of Ohio River bedstone and turning the room into a bar. This led to an argument with the Health Department, which refused to grant an "A" inspection rating because of the ancient floor. Mrs. Dick thought, "Who wanted their damned old 'A' card, anyway?" And she operated the Old House for thirty-two years without it, until the Health Department finally surrendered.

Mrs. Dick moved her first chef, Frenchman George Magnier, to Louisville and opened the restaurant in 1946. Things did not go smoothly from the

Old House and staff. *Courtesy of University of Louisville.*

start. Magnier became lonely for other French folk and went back to New York. Then the remaining employees went on strike. Mrs. Dick remembered how her "life became a rat-race. If a cook didn't show up, I cooked; if the porter didn't come to work, I swept. If the bartender got drunk, I tended bar."

Mrs. Dick wrote her first menu by hand and continued doing this for the next thirty or so years. The menu was "small at first, but [it] had items on it that had never been served in Louisville before nor since." It included pompano

Bauer's sign. *Courtesy of John Nation.*

Mazzoni's-style rolled oysters. *Michelle Turner.*

Left: Vienna Building, 1970s. *Courtesy of Library of Congress.*

Below: Jennie Benedict–style luncheon rolls. *Michelle Turner.*

Jennie Benedict's grave, Cave Hill. *Michelle Turner.*

Site of Canary Cottage. *Michelle Turner.*

Fourth Street postcard, with the Blue Boar Cafeteria on the left, circa 1942. *Courtesy of University of Kentucky.*

Blue Boar–style Salisbury steak. *Michelle Turner.*

Above: Stebbins Grill postcard.
Courtesy of University of Kentucky.

Right: Swizzle postcard. *Courtesy of Boston Public Library.*

Site of Swizzle. *Michelle Turner.*

Kaelin's sign. *Stephen Hacker.*

Above: Hasenour's. *Courtesy of John Nation.*

Right: Leo's Hideaway postcard. *Courtesy of University of Kentucky.*

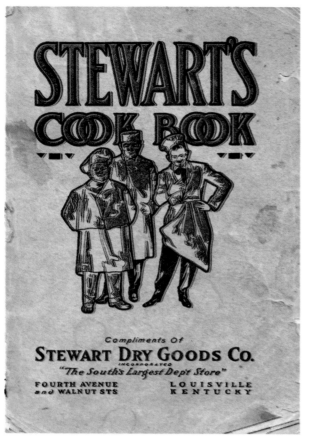

Left: Stewart's Cook Book.
Courtesy of Kathy Cary.

Below: Hick's postcard.
Courtesy of University of Louisville.

Southwind postcard. *Courtesy of Boston Public Library.*

George Leong at Hoe Kow. *Courtesy of Laura Leong.*

Above: Hoe Kow–style war sui gai. *Michelle Turner*.

Left: Ferd Grisanti and sons. *Courtesy of John Nation*.

Left: Derby-Pie®, created at the Melrose Inn. *Michelle Turner*.

Below: Longchamps' rendering of a L'il Abner's. *Courtesy of Denis Kitchen*.

Above: Jay's sign. *Michelle Turner*.

Right: Sixth Avenue in its Mexican/
Southwest phase. *Courtesy of John Nation*.

Left: "That is not I. It is Julia." –Nancy Shepherd. *Stephen Hacker.*

Below: Afro-German Tea Room–style apple crisp. *Michelle Turner.*

Miguel and Maggie de la Torre.
Courtesy of John Nation.

De la Torre's paella. *Courtesy of
John Nation.*

Above: Tim Barnes
(suited) at Timothy's
with chef James Aydlett.
Courtesy of John Nation.

Left: Deitrich's. *Courtesy
of John Nation.*

Right: Deitrich's menu.
Courtesy of Bim Deitrich.

Below: Deitrich's. *Courtesy of Bim Deitrich.*

en papillote, sea bass Chinoise, "Paupiettes of Halibut Jacqueline," broiled shad roe, oysters Rockefeller and pressed duck, often made with recipes she had gleaned from her trips. The pressed duck was quite a show, taking "three waiters to prepare it at tableside in chafing dishes." The food, as former *Courier-Journal* editor Keith Runyon remembers it, was fine: "It wasn't great by any stretch of the imagination according to our current standards. I think one of the specialties of the house was 'Chicken Breast Eugenie,' which was a chicken breast covered with canned peaches or apricots and a thick cream sauce. It wasn't bad. The crêpes were better."

The restaurant boasted a "really fine collection of Rare old whiskies, liquors and wines," many made before Prohibition, presented by guests. Mrs. Dick had "Uncle Sam" evaluate the liquors and attach "regulation tax stamps" so she could "put them on [the] menu at $25, $50 and $100 per drink." She was amazed that "a few damn fools ordered them." Mrs. Dick, who "wouldn't have dreamed of opening" the antique bottles, always managed to be "out" of whatever was asked for.

In 1947, Duncan Hines gave the Old House "a very good recommendation" in his Travel Guide. Over the next two decades, the restaurant continued to attract national notice, receiving an award from *Ford Times*, a magazine published by Ford Motor Company, and getting mentions in the *Saturday Evening Post*, *House Beautiful*, *Esquire* and *Holiday*.

Mrs. Dick continued to creatively avoid any regulations affecting her trade. When the Health Department declined the wrapping she was using as a sufficient sneeze guard for her buffet, Mrs. Dick alerted the manufacturer that the "Louisville Health Department did not accept their cellophane as a sanitary food covering," which caused the manufacturer to pressure the department to back off. The Kentucky Alcoholic Beverage Commission forbade offering free food at bars to stimulate drinking, so Mrs. Dick persuaded famous Louisville potter Mary Alice Hadley to create a ceramic cat vase printed with the legend "Hors-d'Oeuvres, One Cent." Mrs. Dick filled the vase with pennies and placed it on a tray full of snacks, pre-paying for her happy, drink-ready customers. She also proposed a steel-framed canopy for the restaurant, with support posts in the sidewalk. The city wanted the canopy without the posts, and a battle began. Mrs. Dick fought the city through the state's highest court, which ruled against her, and vowed she'd take the matter to the U.S. Supreme Court in 1960. She did not, and she eventually put up the canopy without the posts.

The Old House became the place to bring Derby guests, and Mrs. Dick reveled in the appearance of celebrities such as Walt Disney, Don Ameche and

Old House entryway. *Michelle Turner.*

Ronald Reagan. Governors, bank presidents, mayors and "other high muck-de-mucks" made the Old House their regular stop. She also courted the nearby Catholic church, hosting "Monsignors, Archbishops, priests and a sprinkling of nuns." Keith Runyon describes the downstairs bar as "a bit like the lower level room at 21 Club in New York City," on which he suspects the place was modeled.

In 1963, Mrs. Dick opened the Old House Epicurian next door to her restaurant, selling bottles and jars of the Old House dressings and sauces.

The shop also offered imported cheeses, "unusual" meats and other gourmet foods, again bringing a bit more "Continental" cuisine to Louisville. She wrote two cookbooks and an autobiographical account of her restaurant, which she continued to run according to her own rules—which meant no children were welcome because "a gourmet restaurant is no place for children." Celebrities and luminaries continued to come, weddings and anniversaries were celebrated and Mrs. Dick continued to oversee it all.

Then, as she told the *Courier-Journal* in 1979, Mrs. Dick decided she "was almost 70 years old and…tired." The final days of her Old House were a whirlwind of customers both old and new, wanting (sometimes literally) to get a piece of the restaurant's final days. The newspaper reported that "some of the hundreds of menus from restaurants around the world that decorated the walls of the downstairs dining room…vanished along with Old House menus." A "picture of model Cheryl Tiegs" disappeared from the walls it shared with "the likes of former diners Gerald Ford, Tex Ritter, Raymond Burr, George 'Goober' Lindsey, Cesar Romero and Miss Americas." At midnight on January 31, 1979, Mrs. Dick closed the Old House, went upstairs to her lovely apartment and sat down in a rocking chair.

Several months later, Edward Brockman Jr., a local attorney, leased the restaurant space from Mrs. Dick, buying "all of the furniture and fixtures," including what autographed photos hadn't been lifted during the closing days of the original restaurant. But, as Mrs. Dick said, "it was certainly no longer the Old House." Brockman and his partners removed the building's plaster walls ("some of them…held together only by wallpaper" he told the *Louisville Times*) and much of the old kitchen equipment. They replaced the plumbing and wiring; put in new carpets, paint and wallpaper; and waited for the old business to return. It didn't, and the restaurant went under a few years later.

In 1987, the business was reopened under new ownership and renamed Chez Gemini at the Old House. At the time, Mrs. Dick (who still owned the building) told the *Courier-Journal* she was "thrilled the Old House will reopen," adding, "We had a national reputation. I hope it can again."

Chez Gemini lasted for much of its ten-year lease, closing in 1995 and leaving the building vacant and up for sale. Erma Dick died in 2002, but her awning still stands on Fifth Street—a symbol of the independent and in-your-face woman who made the old building a Louisville icon.

Chapter 24

STEWART'S ORCHID ROOM

White Gloves, Mayonnaise and Murals

S tewart Dry Goods traced its history back to 1846, when a commercial concern known as the New York Store opened on Market Street. But though the store would grow to seven outlets across the metro area before being subsumed by L.S. Ayres in the mid-1980s, Louisville residents' memories of Stewart's center around the store at Fourth Street and Muhammad Ali Boulevard (Walnut Street until 1978). And for many, those memories include an elegant meal in the store's sixth-floor tearoom, known almost since it opened as the Orchid Room.

Stewart's first opened in 1907 and was renovated by 1938 when Roy Wilkinson arrived as food supervisor. Wilkinson opened a basement cafeteria and promoted the store restaurant as a way for people to feel they could eat out and shop on a skimpy Depression-era budget. In the boom years after World War II, Stewart's kept the basement Luncheonette but also expanded the store and opened a 144-seat, leather- and mirror-bedecked "first class restaurant" on the sixth floor, to be called the Tearoom. But, according to *Stewart's: A Louisville Landmark*, "Miss Fetzner, the store's interior decorator, was promoting South American design at the time the Tearoom opened. She decorated the border of one of the new restaurant's mirrors with hand-painted orchids, like the ones found along the Amazon River in Brazil. Her work caught the eyes of both employees and customers who began to refer to the Tearoom as the 'Orchid Room.'"

The Orchid Room became a destination of its own. Keith Runyon, former editor of the *Courier-Journal*, remembers it as an "almost precious experience" involving "ladies with hats and gloves and their dressed-up children." Runyon, who admits to being one of those dressed-up children, said that, from a child's perspective, "the worst part was the service was so slow." Adult Runyon believes that "maybe that was part of the elegance of it all—you weren't being rushed." Unhurried service may indeed been a part of the restaurant's working order, as Stewart's had built its reputation on an "image of gentility," with advertising in newspapers' society sections and salespeople discouraged from crowding or pressuring customers. (It could have also been because the Orchid Room's kitchen was several floors below, in the store's basement.)

With silverware bearing the Stewart's logo (a lion and "1846") and cloth napkins on china-set cloth placemats, the Orchid Room served hot and cold consommés; hot lunches, such as flaked turkey and spaghetti; various cold salads; and sandwiches. A "Neptune Salad Platter" featuring tuna, crabmeat, shrimp "and relishes with assorted petite sandwiches" was often on the menu. Runyon describes the date-nut bread with cream cheese as "a real delicacy" and remembers "peppermint ice cream with hot fudge sauce and real whipped cream." A wide selection of teas was available.

Susan Reigler, former *Courier-Journal* food critic, says she was part of the generation that "had to put on white gloves to go down to shop at Stewart's." But, instead of the Orchid Room, her family usually had lunch in the basement, which was a more informal alternative. Reigler recalls the basement Luncheonette as "sort of a soda fountain or lunch counter, though it had tables, too." In Reigler's memory, Stewart's homemade mayonnaise, which bound various salads, was "delicious" with a "tiny green cast," though the only recorded recipe includes nothing that would so tint it. Runyon remembers the Luncheonette being decorated with a mural of a "country scene with a big tree in the front." In his memory, "The tree changed colors with the season. In the wintertime there was snow, in fall golden leaves… Apparently they went through every season. Somebody stayed late the night before the season changed and changed the mural."

Stewart's basement was also home to the Rebel Room, which Runyon believes was opened around 1961 "at the time of the Civil War Centennial." The Rebel Room had "a stylish cut-out of a couple of Confederate soldiers" placed at the entrance to what the store informed people was "a men's grill," aimed at busy executives who needed their lunches more quickly than the elegant ladies in the Orchid Room or the regular folks in the Luncheonette. As the first man to work in an all-women's department at the *Courier-Journal*, Runyon, a busy man himself,

Fourth Street, with Stewart's on right, 1961. *Courtesy of University of Louisville.*

decided to take his co-workers to lunch at the Rebel Room in 1972. Soon after that, the "men's only" sign was removed.

Racial desegregation had arrived earlier than gender desegregation, though not as quickly as some would have liked. Kenneth Miller wrote that, for many years, "blacks didn't expect to eat in either the Orchid Room or the Luncheonette," and African American employees were expected to serve white workers at store functions. In 1959, civil rights pioneer Dr. Lyman

T. Johnson sat at the Luncheonette, "though he was served only a glass of water." However, by the mid-1960s, Stewart's had relaxed its restrictions, allowing minorities to use all company facilities and admitting them to the Orchid Room.

The Orchid Room's waitresses continued their slow, elegant pace through this change, with many of the women (there were no male waiters at the Orchid Room) building a loyal customer base over the years. One, Lucille Loebig, went so far as to visit a customer's home for a month, administering the lady's insulin shots before she came to work, refusing any payment for her assistance. A cashier, Nora Renshaw, told Miller she "used to greet the customers with 'I'm so glad to see you today,'" adding, "If I knew they had a doctor's appointment, I'd say to them, 'I hope you get a good report.'" The waitresses wore neatly starched uniforms, hairnets and shined shoes, remembering to "serve from the left, clear from the right" and to always pull back a lady's chair.

By the 1980s, as global pressures grew on the nation's department stores, Stewart's began to suffer. Chef Hayward "Haywood" Miller, who oversaw the Orchid Room and the Luncheonette, reported that management "began to suggest instant potatoes, soups, pies and gravy" as part of the store's "cost-cutting measures." On the last day of October in 1985, Stewart's employees were invited to the Orchid Room and told the store was merging with Indianapolis' L.S. Ayres. After changing the name and altering forever Louisvillians' perception of the once-vibrant corner, Ayres sold the former Stewart's to the Hess's chain in 1987.

The Orchid Room and the Luncheonette closed during Ayres' tenure in 1986. Hess's shuttered the downtown store in 1990. The property has risen again as an Embassy Suites hotel. It offers a free cooked-to-order breakfast, "light appetizers and great conversation" at a complimentary evening reception, plus "fine dining featuring steak and seafood" at Catch 23. But the "special world" remembered by Runyon and Reigler—the elegant Art Deco world of white gloves and ladies who lunch—is gone forever.

CHICKEN TETRAZZINI

Adapted from *Stewarts: A Louisville Landmark*. Serves six.

Early in the twentieth century, before it had restaurants, Stewart Dry Goods published a cookbook. Kenneth L. Miller wrote that his father and the other Stewart's kitchen staff had few written recipes, and customers' and the local newspapers' requests for recipes were always politely declined. Chef Miller provided his son with a few recipes for the latter's 1991 book. This adaptation uses substantially less than the called-for two pounds each of chicken and country ham, which one can only assume was a mistake of memory or a typographical error.

7 tablespoons butter (divided)
1 small onion, diced
½ pound mushrooms, sliced
1 cup country ham, cooked and diced
2 cups poached or roast chicken meat, cut into small pieces
4 tablespoons flour
2 cups chicken stock
1 cup heavy cream
2 tablespoons dry sherry
black pepper
2 tablespoons chopped parsley
8 ounces dried "fine noodles" (e.g., thin fettuccine), boiled and drained
grated Parmesan cheese

Melt 2 tablespoons butter in a large skillet. Add onions and cook over medium-low heat for 3–4 minutes, stirring. Add another tablespoon of butter, then mushrooms. Cook mushrooms for a couple minutes, tossing, then add ham. When mushrooms are cooked through, add chicken and cook just until chicken is warmed. Remove from heat and set aside.

Melt 4 tablespoons butter in a saucepan. Add flour, whisking for a couple minutes until incorporated and cooked. Slowly add stock, whisking. After stock is incorporated, slowly add cream, continuing to whisk. Add sherry and a generous amount of pepper. Cook, stirring with a whisk, until sauce has thickened. Stir in parsley.

Pour white sauce over meat/mushroom mixture in skillet. Stir. Taste for seasoning and add salt and more pepper if needed.

Place cooked noodles in six buttered gratin dishes or one buttered large shallow baking dish. Distribute sauce over noodles.

Sprinkle with a generous amount of Parmesan cheese. Brown under broiler (about 8 inches from heating element).

Chapter 25

C-54 GRILL

The Restaurant that Got its Wings

As early as 1943, years before victory in World War II, the U.S. government began studying what to do for veterans returning from their service and how surplus war materiel might be handled. The first "GI Bill" created many benefits for veterans, among them education, training and loan guarantees for homes, farms and businesses. Another government program, the Surplus War Property Administration, was busy finding a way to sell over $100 billion of unneeded war materiel. How these government programs benefited veterans and others crystallized in the form of Louisville's Herman Weist and his C-54 Grill.

In 1948, Weist told a reporter that he came up with the idea while he was watching PBY seaplanes operate in the Pacific when he served in the navy during the war. He said, "Those Navy patrol planes had everything aboard….Refrigerator, water, tables, windows and even rest rooms. If all that could be crowded into a plane the size of a PBY…I thought a large plane would make a good restaurant."

When Weist got out of the navy, he began his search for a surplus plane. Spotting an ad from a plant in Arkansas, he decided to buy a C-54 Skymaster. The military version of the Douglass DC-4 commercial transport, the Skymaster was ninety-four feet long and just over twenty-seven feet high and served various functions during the war, including one specially designed to transport Franklin Roosevelt to the Yalta Conference.

Weist and a crew took the wings off the plane "while sparks flew and rivets popped" and then loaded the fuselage on train flat cars for the trip to

The only known photo of the C-54 Grill, badly damaged. *Courtesy of University of Louisville.*

Louisville. Weist put the C-54 on a brick-and-cement foundation, painted the plane's original soundproof material blue and silver and ran fluorescent lights down the ceiling. He installed restrooms, air conditioning and a counter and built cabinets covered by stainless steel doors.

What did Weist's diner, located near the corner of Lexington Road and Grinstead Drive, serve? A newspaper reported in 1948 that the plane's crew section was where Weist placed a small kitchen for "peeling potatoes and smashing hamburger," and "the only wings…[the plane] has left are on the fried chicken dinner." It may have been popular with Louisville veterans, and the tall fuselage may have made an impressive sight in 1948, but the C-54 Grill only stayed in Louisville for a few years—not because it was unpopular, but because the Skymaster was needed for another service.

In 1951, the Associated Press reported the unusual news that a "Louisville restaurant soon will be flying the Pacific." It seems the C-54 Grill had been sold to "a small, unidentified airline that operates from Seattle to Tokyo by way of Alaska." Weist told the reporter that the Grill would be "taken to a western aircraft plant, [and] fitted with wings, tail assembly, engines and controls. Then it will be put into service." The report intimated that "high prices and the difficulty of obtaining new planes" had initiated the return of C-54 Grill to the skies.

According to his obituary, Weist "was a man of many interests and many careers." He became a prominent Louisville "businessman, inventor, film producer and yacht builder." Weist held "many patents for sophisticated medical equipment and innovative plastic bag manufacturing machinery" and was a loving father and grandfather. However, the obituary did not mention what may be Weist's greatest accomplishment—creating a Louisville restaurant that managed, literally, to fly away.

Chapter 26
HICK'S, SOUTHWIND AND PRYORS

Leading Louisville into the Postwar Suburbs

B y the 1940s, automobiles had brought great changes to Louisville, and restaurants were beginning to adapt. Cunningham's began offering drive-in service by 1942, but wartime limits on gas and food meant many establishments had to wait for victory. When the war ended, the boom was on. The energy and optimism of postwar America was reflected in the rise of automobile culture and in modern styles of architecture, including the dramatic "visual front" style emphasizing glass panes showcasing clean interiors. The postwar years were a good time for Louisville as roads, homes and new employment opportunities abounded.

As people moved away from downtown, restaurants sprang up to meet them, many offering convenient drive-in service for suburban motorists. One such place was Hick's Drive-in Restaurant, "one mile south of Shively on Dixie Highway." Hick's opened in the 1947, offering twenty-four-hour-a-day curb service for "Steaks, Chops and Chicken Dinners" and breakfast at any hour.

The available images show that Hick's was an example of early American modernist roadside design. While gleaming and modern on the inside, Hick's exterior featured awnings and other details designed to give it a more "regional" feel. Much more modernist were the Southwind Drive-In, also on Dixie Highway, and Pryors Restaurant on Shelbyville Road at South Hubbards Lane.

The Southwind straddled the late 1940s and early 1950s as a simple, square restaurant with a glass front, almost dwarfed by the enormous letters spelling "SOUTHWIND RESTAURANT" on top. A 1954 *Louisville Times* "Dining

Hick's interior. *Courtesy of University of Louisville.*

Guide" reported that, like Hick's, Southwind never closed: "Anytime of the day or night you can get delicious hamburgers, steaks, chops and chicken. Curb service available from 6:00 to 1:00. Whether you're in the mood for a snack in your car or a dinner inside, try the Southwind."

Pryors in St. Matthews embraced the Modernist "visual front" aesthetic with a building that seemed to be made almost entirely of glass. Its beige brick surfaces were covered with large signs advertising steakburgers, steaks, shakes and "breakfast service," overseen by a glowing yellow stick figure striding ahead with a serving tray.

It's unclear what happened to the Hick's and Southwind sites, though other automobile-friendly fast food places may very well occupy their spaces on Dixie Highway. Pryors suffered a more dramatic end. In 1957, a gas explosion injured several people, including a kitchen helper who was hurled twenty-five feet from the building. William Wilson told an AP reporter: "I smelled gas and the next thing I knew I was sitting out in the middle of Hubbards Lane." The report did not mention what happened to the neon-lit stick man.

Chapter 27

MELROSE INN

From Attracting Motorists to Owning the Derby

U.S. Route 42 has run from Cleveland to Louisville since about the time America started to seriously get into automobiles. Once the main thoroughfare between Cincinnati and Louisville, Route 42 offered an irresistible opportunity to Oldham County farmers, who beckoned travelers by building restaurants, motels and roadhouses as early as the 1930s. Places such as the Ashbourne Inn and the Chicken Trail Inn offered souvenirs, southern specialties like country ham and places to stay.

As the car culture continued to grow, around the middle of the twentieth century, Ann and Jack Smiser, both raised in Oldham County, decided to get in on the action. The couple opened a motel on nine acres near the Oldham/Jefferson line in Prospect, naming it after "a plantation called Melrose" they had seen on a trip to Natchez, Mississippi. The motel began with thirty rooms and soon grew to fifty-six, advertising itself as the "South's Finest" and "Louisville's finest suburban motor court." Postcards called out the "lovely Kentucky bluegrass scenery, 9-½ miles from the noises of the city."

By the 1960s, in addition to "radios and television," "steam heat" and "cross ventilation," the Melrose proudly advertised that the adjoining restaurant served "fine food better." Nancy Theiss, of the Oldham County History Center, said in a 2010 interview that "Ann [Smiser] created an environment of southern hospitality for visitors, serving up traditional Kentucky food favorites such as country ham and biscuits and minted juleps." Jenny Ballard, who began working at the Melrose as a dishwasher around 1970 when she was just twelve, remembers cooking "chicken livers, beef liver and

Mr. Kern making pie at the Melrose Inn. *Courtesy of Alan Rupp.*

onions and fried chicken" after she grew old enough to help with the menu preparation. (She also remembers having to "stand on a wooden Coca-Cola crate to be tall enough to reach the dishwasher.") Ballard, who describes herself as the Melrose's "jack of all trades," remembers a particular group of regulars the servers referred to as "the liar's table." "It was all farmers," she says. "They would stay in there for three or four hours telling stories to each other, to us, to anyone who would listen to them." In addition to

Oldham county lore, locals and visitors alike could also enjoy the Melrose's complimentary relish tray, featuring apple butter, cottage cheese and carrot and celery sticks.

Because of its charms (and perhaps its complimentary relish tray), the Melrose became a popular destination for travelers and Louisville residents alike, especially around Derby time. And one of the reasons was a chocolate-nut-bourbon confection that became known as Derby-Pie®. The now-famous (and trademarked) pie was developed by Walter and Leaudra Kern, who were on their way to Florida in 1954 when they stopped in Louisville to help their daughter before grandson Alan Rupp was born. The Kerns wound up taking over the Melrose operation from the Smisers. Looking for a signature dessert, they came up with several names, selecting "Derby Pie" by literally pulling it out of a hat. The dessert was a huge hit. Rupp, now president of Kern's Kitchen, Inc., remembers his grandparents telling stories "about a customer who would come down from Cincinnati to the Melrose just for the Derby Pie." Rupp remembers that it was "Mr. Ed [Hasenour]" who recommended that the Kerns "get the Derby Pie name trademarked." They did, and soon Derby-Pie® became the Kerns' main business.

The Kerns left the Melrose, and despite the "Home of Derby Pie" sign that remained at the motel, the dessert was no longer an Oldham County exclusive. The Melrose closed around 2000. The site where the Kerns' pie was invented is now a self-serve gas and food mart, serving exurban commuters over the faint echoes from nearby interstate highways. But, even after I-71 opened in the 1970s, as traffic dwindled on the old Route 42, Rupp still remembers delivering pies to the Melrose kitchen and the "bunch of old country ladies cooking good country food" who welcomed everyone to one of Oldham county's most legendary inns.

Chapter 28

LI'L ABNER'S

Dogpatch Comes "Home"

Before Sadie Hawkins Days, before the "double whammy" and definitely before there were beatniks or Daisy Duke, there was Al Capp and Li'l Abner. According to the *New York Times* obituary, Capp was born Alfred Gerald Caplin in 1909. In 1934, he debuted a comic strip featuring "an entirely naive 19-year-old hillbilly" from a "never-never land without indoor plumbing." The strip was built on biting satire and poked fun at celebrities, other comics and politicians. Abner Yokum; his parents, Mammy and Pappy; buxom love interest Daisy Mae; Lonesome Polecat; Joe Btfsplk; and other characters visiting Dogpatch had tens of millions of fans flocking to Capp's daily strip, films, Broadway shows and more. Denis Kitchen, coauthor of *Al Capp: A Life to the Contrary*, says that, in addition to penning his daily strip, Capp was "a TV personality, a radio personality, a bon vivant." Hailed as "the greatest humorist of his day" and ranked with Mark Twain and Charles Dickens as a serious artist, Capp did admit that, when he started "Li'l Abner," his goal was not to become a literary lion but to "modify his diet by being able to afford three square meals a day." This may explain why Capp had many licensing deals and why, for several years, Louisville had a Li'l Abner's restaurant.

Louisville's Li'l Abner's began as an idea of Richard D. Cleaves, a sales manager for Continental Can Company. Cleaves had helped develop the first Li'l Abner's drive-in in Illinois before arriving in Louisville in 1957. Located at the juncture of Lexington Road and Grinstead Drive, later the site of Jim Porter's, the structure was described as having a swaybacked "hillbilly motif" with a giant sign featuring Li'l Abner "hisself" looming over it.

Keith Runyon, former editor of the *Courier-Journal*, remembers "a lot of political incorrectness about it," but also that the restaurant was very popular, with an "old-fashioned wooden swing made of kind of big long pine pulls with a very rustic looking bench" where kids would swing while waiting outside. According to a *Louisville Times* article about an initial stock offering for "Dogpatch, Inc.," the restaurant could seat 150 people in its dining room and provide curb service for fifty cars. With Mr. Cleaves as president, Dogpatch, Inc. said it planned "a chain of Li'l Abner restaurants under a franchise from Al Capp Enterprises, Inc."

Based on ephemera from the Morton Grove, Illinois outlet and confirmed by native Louisvillians who remember the local Li'l Abner's, the restaurant served a variety of "scrumptious vittles," including "Hammus Alabamus," "Presarved Turnips" and "Fried Chicken Yokum Style with all the Trimmin's." There was also "Kickapoo Joy Juice," a beverage Runyon describes as "kind of a watermelon juice" that was "the nastiest thing" he's ever tasted. Servers were dressed as "Dogpatch characters," delivering "Chuck Buckets filled to the brim with delicious & tasty Yokumburgers." The menu also offered a "Salomey Dog," "Li'l Abner's Speshul Pride Steak" and "Stupefyin' Jones Sundaes." It was filled with Capp characters, with the author himself appearing to accept "apologies…and permission" of the restaurant.

Runyon does not recall "Stupifyin' Jones," but he and others do remember a mammoth ice cream concoction called the "Big Stanislaus," named after yet another of Capp's innumerable Dogpatch characters. It's unclear whether the "Big Stanislaus" had thirty-two scoops of ice cream, whether it had sparklers or even if it was an ice cream soda. What everyone does agree on is that the child brave enough to stuff himself silly could earn "a brass plaque" on Li'l Abner's wall.

In 1968, the *New York Times* announced that "Li'l Abner, Daisy Mae and several other Al Capp comic characters" would "become part of the burgeoning franchised fast-food roadside restaurant business" of Longchamps, Inc., a "New York–based diversified restaurant concern." Making no mention of any previous Li'l Abner's restaurants, Longchamps promised "'Hamus Alabamus' barbecued sandwiches, and 'Mammy Yokum' fried chicken" in a building representing "a typical structure in Dogpatch."

Runyon remembers when Louisville's Li'l Abner's ran into "licensing problems," saying the restaurant owners "changed the name to Big

Longchamps' rendering of a L'il Abner's. *Courtesy of Denis Kitchen.*

Abner's, which was supposed to solve the problem." But it "didn't have the charm of Li'l Abner's," and there may have been deeper reasons than the licensing issues, as Longchamps did not remain in business much longer. Runyon observes that, for Capp and his characters, "the demographics were changing" in the late 1960s: "All those little kids who had been swinging at Li'l Abner's were now hopping in their rods and going to Frisch's and…the other drive-ins."

Chapter 29

HOE KOW

Bringing Louisville "Something Exotic"

Ask almost any Louisvillian of a certain age about his favorite Chinese food, and he will undoubtedly mention the war sui gai from Hoe Kow. When the restaurant closed in 1995, one customer was "mourning" the dish after eating it three times during Hoe Kow's last week, telling the *Courier-Journal*, "Nobody makes Cantonese food like they do." No one would argue that the Leongs' menu didn't offer Cantonese cuisine—but one can argue that the dish Louisville loves most from this long-lasting restaurant was more Motown than mainland China.

Canton, now known as Guangdong, was the region producing some of the earliest Chinese Americans, many of whom began to arrive in California in the mid-1800s and began spreading out across the United States soon thereafter. Barred from many avenues of employment by discriminatory practices, many Chinese immigrants started restaurants, giving Americans a baseline idea of what Chinese cuisine should be by using the name of their province's main city, Canton. According to John Mariani, "chop suey" appeared in American newspapers as early as 1888, and by 1914, proto-foodies were sneering that signs advertising the signature Chinese American dish smacked of inauthenticity, as "one seldom sees a Chinaman eating in the restaurants that are most attractive to Americans." Mariani credited "Chinese cooks who fed the workers on the Pacific railroad lines" in the late nineteenth century, disputing the claim that the name comes from the Mandarin phrase meaning "a little of this and a little of that." Whatever the true origin of chop suey, "Cantonese" cuisine caught on in America. By

1928, Louisville had its own chop suey house, the Liberty Inn, and a small but growing population of Chinese residents.

In 1933, Laura "Lolly" Woo-Sang was born in Louisville, spending her first years in her family's home above a laundry at Fifth and Broadway. "We lived where Kupie's restaurant was," she remembers, saying her family was forced to leave the building when she was six or seven years old. She recalls playing with the children of the Canines, the dentists living in the building that would become Erma Dick's Old House Restaurant. When Laura was growing up in Louisville, "there were only about one hundred Chinese people here." Laura was allowed to speak only Chinese at home, as her mother never learned English and she and her four siblings "were supposed to know Chinese" in order to be able to speak to their grandmother when they "saw her in China"—a visit that sadly never happened. The children did well in school, with Laura's elder brother becoming valedictorian of his class at Manual High School. After attending Ahrens Trade School, Laura became a legal secretary. But her mother, a Chinese immigrant from Kowloon, thought it was time for Laura to marry.

Laura, the youngest of five children, said she was a "change of life baby," adding that her mother claimed "she could die in peace if only someone would come and marry her old maid daughter." Mother Woo-Sang's prayers were answered with the arrival of George Leong, an accountant from Detroit. George and Laura were married and, by 1961, were anticipating a baby and a move to Chicago, where George was already working. But once Laura's parents "saw their first grandchild, there was no more talk of leaving Louisville." Laura remembers asking George, who could not find accounting work in Louisville, "What can you do?" and hearing him reply, "I can cook." George told Laura that he had worked in restaurants in Detroit after arriving there from China at age ten.

In 1962, the Leongs found a ready-to-inhabit space at Bowman Field, where someone named Jimmy Lynn had "left the chairs, tables and everything" from a former restaurant at the site that was once "several administration offices." The small space with its "institutional, Central State green" décor was decorated with plants, Chinese prints and paintings. The Leongs, leaving their infant son with his delighted grandparents, began the hard work of bringing another Chinese restaurant to Louisville. Laura remembers George being "gone every day from 11 a.m. to 11 p.m.," with the front-of-house duties making her hours slightly shorter. "I'd get my son up about 11 or 11:30 at night and say: 'This is your father!'"

Bowman Field, site of Hoe Kow. *Michelle Turner.*

Many attribute Hoe Kow's early success to Louisville's Jewish community, centered, as it was, around Taylorsville Road. Laura says that, while she later heard Chinese restaurateurs often recommend locating in Jewish neighborhoods, the Leongs "just happened to luck out" as their decision was mostly based on the restaurant-ready facility. But, in a nod to the neighborhood, since people would often ask about pork and ham, chicken soup was always Hoe Kow's "soup of the day." Not that religious tradition could stop all enjoyment of what Hoe Kow had on offer. The restaurant's egg rolls, made with leftover barbecued pork and rolled by hand in the kitchen, came with every Hoe Kow dinner. Laura Leong says one frequent diner would "have her egg drop soup, which we had every day for the Jewish people, and the egg roll that came with it. She would eat a couple of bites, then ask the waitress if it had pork. When the waitress answered 'yes,' she would act shocked and put it down. She did this every time she came in."

The Leongs continued to grow the audience for Hoe Kow's Chinese food through the 1960s and '70s. George worked busily in the kitchen while Laura handled the staff, who stayed with them for decades due to Laura's diplomatic handling of George's outbursts. "George is a very introverted person," Laura says, "but in that restaurant, boy, was he loud." The waitstaff "all said we were the nicest people they ever worked for, but I told them, 'I can't believe it with George hollering at you like that!'"

Former *Louisville Times* reviewer Richard Des Ruisseaux remembers Hoe Kow as one of the restaurants that helped make Louisville dining "a little more daring." In a 1972 write-up, Des Ruisseaux described Hoe Kow as "one of…[his] favorite restaurants, and a lot of other people's, too." In 1974, the Leongs remodeled the always-crowded Bowman Field space, adding tables, hiding the New Deal–era ductwork with black paint, muffling kitchen noise with "mini-shag carpeting of orange, green and gold" and hanging Chinese lanterns from the ceiling. In 1979, as the airport leasing board argued over their rent, the Leongs decided to move Hoe Kow to their own building in Middletown.

In his 1972 review, Des Ruisseaux noted that he liked his lobster tail Cantonese but made himself "full to overflowing" by oversampling his wife's war sui gai. Even after Hoe Kow's move to Middletown, the "Chinese fried chicken" remained the restaurant's "most popular dish, with moo goo steak kew…the runner up." In a 2014 column, Louisville food writer Ron Mikulak recalled that, when he fielded recipe requests for the *Courier-Journal*'s "Cook's Corner" column, one of the most persistent requests he was "unable to satisfy" was for Hoe Kow's war sui gai. When Mikulak answered that "war su gai is a relatively common preparation in American Chinese restaurants, and that there are likely many versions of the dish available in cookbooks or on the Internet," he was "lambasted for suggesting that any such variation could be as wonderful as the one crafted by the Hoe Kow kitchen." Readers went so far as to suggest that if Mikulak wasn't "so lazy," he "could trace down the recipe and provide it." Mikulak's "boilerplate" response to the many war sui gai requests was

There was likely no "recipe" as such, that the cooks at Hoe Kow were very likely trained by doing (likely by their parents); that their English-language proficiencies likely prohibited them from explaining, let alone writing down, how they made the dish; that they very likely used very high temperature woks that a home kitchen could not match; that their ingredients were likely obtained from suppliers not available to a home retail customer; and that the real reason that this dish stands out in Louisvillians' memories is that the cooks made it twenty times a night, seven nights a week, and had it down pat; and, very likely, it was one of the first "exotic" restaurant meals that the diner had enjoyed.

Mikulak was certainly right about the high-temperature woks and the seven nights a week of work. But war sui gai is neither common in American Chinese kitchens nor is it actually Chinese. It's a regional American dish that very likely originated in Detroit, where George Leong learned to cook.

Catering to the American palate, Cantonese restaurant cooks added deep-fried dishes with starchier breading and sweeter sauces than Chinese people would usually prefer. As the chefs spread across the country, adaptations were made to local tastes. One of these was war sui gai, known around Columbus, Ohio, and Detroit as "almond boneless chicken" or "ABC." Boneless chicken breasts are dipped into a thick, tempura-style batter and then deep-fried until golden brown. Cut on the diagonal, the fried chicken pieces are set on shredded iceberg lettuce. Brown mushroom gravy is drizzled over the top and then sprinkled with almonds and green onions. Vegetables such as celery, bamboo shoots or water chestnuts might be added, depending on one's location. Unlike chop suey, chow mein and egg foo yung, which began in New York and spread everywhere, war sui gai stayed mostly confined to the Upper Midwest, with small inroads into a few other states. In Louisville, war sui gai was found at Hoe Kow.

Laura Leong remembers "one of the nicest compliments we got was when friends told us they had gone to another Chinese restaurant and noticed war sui gai on the menu." When the friends asked the waitress if it was true that this restaurant had the dish, according to Laura, the waitress replied, "Yes, we have war sui gai, but it's not like Hoe Kow's." Laura confirmed that George learned to cook war sui gai in Detroit, "but his version was just different from what he had learned as a young man." For one thing, it had snow peas, which are not seen elsewhere. Hoe Kow's war sui gai became so well known that *Gourmet Magazine* called for the recipe, but George refused. To this day, Laura still isn't giving any hints. "I do not cook," she says. "I never even boiled water, and that's the truth." Laura says that, no matter how busy things got, George personally cooked every dish of war sui gai.

The years went by. More Chinese and other Asians moved to the area, and Louisvillians began to experience Hunan and Szechuan cuisine. Feeling "the pressure of all the new restaurants," Hoe Kow added some new items to the menu, but even when Laura "went to every table every night and explained everything on it," people would "get the old standbys." So they changed the menu back. Some critics, however, began to carp. In 1986, David Inman wrote that that, even though "Hoe Kow was Chinese when Chinese wasn't cool," a recent visit had "revealed signs of fading glory." A few years later, Robin Garr said he couldn't include Hoe Kow among his "favorite Chinese restaurants anymore."

Despite the spicier competition, Hoe Kow continued to be popular in Middletown. But in 1995, the Leongs decided that after thirty-two years, they'd had enough. The couple retired, selling the tables, chairs and other fixtures before the property was demolished to make way for a Walgreens. The ornate, Chinese-style arch, where the Leongs "watched children grow up, then bring their children back to eat," was taken down. The waitstaff, some of whom had been with Hoe Kow since the beginning, found other employment. Laura Leong said she looked forward to "the pleasure to do nothing, the choice to do nothing" after working for so long. On May 28, 1995, Hoe Kow closed for good.

These days, the Leongs are still enjoying their retirement. Laura says George made war sui gai once after he retired, but "it did not come out the way he wanted it and he's never made it again." Laura says, "I give my money to the casinos now…My friends and I catch the bus at K-mart." She doesn't eat Chinese food, preferring Italian: "As long as it's got pasta and either a white or red sauce, give it to me." Laura and George may have moved on from Hoe Kow, but Louisville is still in love with war sui gai—and the Detroit-Louisville combination that put the city on the Chinese American food map.

War Sui Gai

Adapted from AmericanFoodRoots.com, which adapted it from a 1979 recipe from the *Detroit Free Press*. Serves four.

4 boneless, skinless chicken breast halves
½ teaspoon kosher salt
1 tablespoon sherry
about 40 snow pea pods, trimmed
1 teaspoon toasted sesame oil
1 teaspoon neutral (e.g., canola) oil, plus additional for frying
1½ cups sliced mushrooms

Sauce:
4 tablespoons cornstarch
3 tablespoons water

3 cups chicken broth
3 tablespoons butter
2 tablespoons soy sauce
1 tablespoon oyster sauce

Batter:
3 tablespoons cornstarch
3 tablespoons flour
½ teaspoon baking powder
1 egg, beaten
1 tablespoon water

To serve:
shredded iceberg lettuce
½ cup slivered almonds, toasted
1 or 2 scallions (green and white parts), thinly sliced

Toss chicken with salt and sherry to coat well. Marinate for at least 15 minutes.

Blanch pea pods in rapidly boiling salted water for a few seconds. Drain in a colander, then shock in ice-cold water. Drain again and set aside.

In a wok or skillet, heat sesame oil and one teaspoon neutral oil. Add mushrooms and stir-fry until done. Remove from heat.

Prepare sauce: In a medium saucepan, mix together the cornstarch and water and stir until smooth. Gradually add the chicken stock, whisking until smooth. Add butter, soy sauce and oyster sauce. Bring mixture to a boil, whisking constantly. Let boil for about a minute, still whisking, until mixture is slightly thickened. Remove from heat. Taste for seasoning, adding more salt if needed.

Prepare batter: In a small bowl, mix together cornstarch, flour and baking powder. Add egg and water and beat with a whisk until smooth.

Heat about 1 inch of neutral oil in a wok or skillet to 375 degrees. Dip chicken breasts in batter to coat. Fry in hot oil until golden, turning as necessary to cook evenly. Remove and drain on a rack or paper towels.

While chicken is draining, warm sauce. Add pea pods to mushroom mixture and reheat, tossing to heat evenly.

Cut chicken diagonally into strips. Place each sliced chicken breast on a bed of shredded lettuce. Spoon sauce over, then top with mushrooms and pea pods. Sprinkle with almonds and scallions.

Chapter 30

SIMMONS

Lowering Cases, Losing Customers

"Mꜳay I count you among those who support the art of culinary in Louisville?" began a 1973 letter from Ray Simmons, a public relations executive seeking "a vote of confidence" in the form of an early reservation for his new restaurant, simmons. "I called it simmons, always with a lower case 's,'" Simmons says. "The *Courier-Journal* always had to put 'lower case 's' intentional.'" Simmons, who had come to Louisville in 1964 from Chicago, formed his own public relations firm in 1973. Simmons's restaurant and PR firm had the same phone number, which Ray recalls as a clever trick: "I would answer the phone 'Simmons,' and if they asked what was on the menu, I knew which…they wanted to talk to." Simmons does not say if there was ever any confusion over the two businesses. He does admit some confusion when it came to running a restaurant. And it's clear that he made some confusing choices about his restaurant's PR.

"My biggest mistake was not knowing anything about running a restaurant," Simmons says. Somehow this did not discourage a circle of investors, allowing simmons to open in a circa-1886 building at 734 South First Street. A 1974 menu describes the restaurant's walls, floors and ceilings as "covered with deep brown fabric and carpet." There were taupe velvet drapes and ivory woodwork with a dark brown glaze. Lighting was "arranged to provide a feeling of being suspended in space and to focus attention on the tables with their bright blue cloths and on the waiters with their matching bright blue formal jackets." The "art of the culinary" was painstakingly detailed:

Menus are planned by Mr. Simmons to take advantage of foods at the peak of their season. Each item is selected for the universality of its flavor appeal, its texture, its color and its compatibility with other foods being served. No substitutions are ever permitted at simmons...Mr. Simmons employs skilled culinary artists, buys the finest ingredients available and demands absolute dedication to perfection in the smallest detail of food preparation and service. Some simmons recipes are entirely original. Most are adaptations of popular French dishes with occasional tributes to the cuisines of Spain, Austria, Japan and Russia.

Patrons with reservations were assured that, "upon ringing the doorbell," they would "be greeted by a handsomely attired butler" who would "take their wraps and usher them into a richly appointed dining room with only three tables." The fourteen-dollar *prix fixe* menu offered "entirely original" dishes such as "pate Beauchamp, celeriac remoulade, skewered sates with peanut sauce, spiced Spanish almonds, onion soup with bourbon flambé" and "quenelle with sauce nantua." The restaurant hoped to attract what it called "the 'in' crowd, people with interesting backgrounds and vocations," the kind of people who "looked at, not leered at" ladies in low-cut dresses.

By early 1975, simmons was noted not for being "Louisville's finest small gourmet restaurant" but for its financial troubles. Acknowledging to

Site of simmons. *Michelle Turner.*

the *Louisville Times* that the restaurant had been in financial difficulty since it opened, "was about out of liquor, and had only $46 in the bank," Ray Simmons nevertheless insisted that it would be successful because there were "still enough Louisvillians with gourmet appetites to make the business grow." (Simmons noted, however, that when he was planning the project, "he got a lot of verbal and moral support and he heard a lot about the need for a gourmet-style restaurant here." But, since the restaurant opened, he "found that Louisville may have more gourmet talkers than eaters.") The restaurant added tables to seat a total of thirty-six people. The *prix fixe* menu price was raised to $16.00 and less costly *à la carte* dinners starting at $5.95 were offered "for the less affluent, less sophisticated customer."

Simmons's approach to reservations (booking seats months in advance but failing to confirm as the date approached) may have contributed to the troubles. "Here I am telling people 'no, we don't have any reservations until next June, or whatever,' and here I'm sitting in an empty restaurant," recalls Simmons. "They…probably forgot about it."

Advertising executive William Beam, a "major stockholder," told this story of the restaurant's troubles to the *Louisville Times*:

> *As few as four people were showing up on week nights* [sic], *not even a crowd in a place that seats only 36 people…Simmons, then manager, had begun calling emergency meetings of stockholders. They would ante up more money to keep the place going…*Louisville Times *restaurant critic, Ann Cooper, showed up. A busboy promptly knocked over a pot of special sauce for the lobster. More was hastily made up. The first serving went to the critic. A story appeared indicating there was nothing good at simmons but the green beans.*

After that, Beam told the reporter, "We hit with a thud." LG&E shut off the lights. The art on the walls was taken down. With no bottled gas for cooking and no money, another "emergency meeting" was held. One stockholder gave a busboy ten dollars to buy candles. Other stockholders (which had initially included Barry Bingham Sr.) brought candles from home. Beam and the chef brought in camper stoves and cooked on them by candlelight. Money was pitched in, wine and spirits were purchased from a nearby liquor store and some investors even helped wash dishes. For the time, simmons stayed open, which Beam attributed to "St. Jude, the patron saint of lost causes."

In a 1976 *Louisville Times* interview, Beam sounded more upbeat about simmons. There was a new chef, Ralph Kattermeier, and a waitstaff captain with a long record of Louisville experience. Ray Simmons was referred to as "a consultant" and "heading a catering service connected to the restaurant." Beam proudly reported "a profit of $296.44" for the month, which was "a far cry from the $7,385.98 loss" the restaurant had suffered in that month a year earlier. The report ended: "The lights are on, the art is back on the walls. There's gas and liquor, and the stockholders at last have hope that this small, quaint little restaurant in the unlikely location is going to make it."

It didn't. The lawyer who has owned the building for the past seventeen years says it was previously occupied by a firm that printed forms, sharing the space with a computer firm. Ray Simmons went back to public relations. The ornamental iron fence is no longer in the front yard, and there is no more "butler-waiter" to admit people to the lowercase restaurant that had such high expectations.

Chapter 31

FERD GRISANTI'S

Plaster Flamingos Foregone for Four-Star Reputation

The Grisanti family came to Louisville in the 1800s, establishing themselves as ornamental plasterers. Grisanti molding can be found on the Pendennis Club, the Seelbach and Brown Hotels and other buildings of the era. By the 1940s, Albert Grisanti and his brother, Ferd, had opened the G.M.G Art and Novelty Co. at 1000 Fehr Street (now East Liberty), turning out religious statues and "nicely finished gift-shop items." But the Eisenhower administration's push for interstate highways meant the roadside tourist stands dotting the smaller state routes were dwindling and backyard Virgin Mary shrines and plaster pink flamingoes weren't going to pay the bills.

Searching for another way to make money, the brothers recalled compliments about the cooking of Albert's wife and their cousin, Dorina Mattei. The Grisantis sold their flamingo molds, remodeled their building, chased out the plaster dust and, in 1959, opened a restaurant. They called it Casa Grisanti. Dorina cooked. Albert was maître d'. Ferd Grisanti worked in the kitchen, did some hosting and tended bar. "We all worked together and worked hard," Ferd told a reporter. While not the first Italian restaurant in Louisville, Casa Grisanti quickly became one of the city's favorites. The brothers were happy the restaurant was successful, but they knew it would be hard to pass the business on to their many children (Ferd had six; Albert had four). In 1971, Ferd sold his one-third share in Casa Grisanti and started looking for a place to open his own restaurant.

Ferd Grisanti's. *Courtesy of John Nation.*

After planning for a couple years, Ferd bought a property far out on Taylorsville Road, in Jeffersontown, opening Ferd Grisanti's Villa Toscana in 1973. The original menu "mirrored Casa Grisanti's," says Paul Grisanti, one of Ferd's sons: "Like Casa Grisanti, we had fried chicken on our menu. But soon we took off the things that weren't really Italian, like the fried chicken. We had marinara, meatballs, a variety of things."

At first, business was a little rough. "I will admit that it was not the best decision to go" to J-town, says Paul. "In hindsight, there just wasn't any traffic there. To give you a measure, today Hurstbourne Lane has six lanes at the intersection with Taylorsville, and has a traffic count of over seventy thousand cars a day. Back then Hurstbourne was two lanes and dead-ended at Taylorsville Road." The downtown Grisantis had begun to shift toward a coat-and-tie dress code and tableside preparation. And the J-town Grisantis realized that the neighbors were making assumptions about their restaurant. "They didn't know us, they didn't come," Paul recalls. "They saw the name and associated us with Casa Grisanti, and they just assumed we were expensive." But Ferd's family persevered, keeping their "different style." Paul Grisanti says, "We were more relaxed. You didn't have to wear a coat and tie."

In 1981, Paul and his brother, Vince, took over restaurant operations from their father, who became host and "ambassador." The younger management did more things to set Ferd's apart from their relatives' fine dining establishment. The brothers enlarged the menu, heightened service and continued to win over their J-town neighbors. Ferd's began an annual Derby buffet and another for the J-town Gaslight Festival. It also advertised with "Ferd Words," which were Italian-pun-based lines like "All the Pasta-bilities."

Ultimately, "the people of J-town really supported us," recalls Paul. What people really came to like was the food. Ferd's made its own meat sauce and fresh pasta. The restaurant described itself in a 1984 ad as striving to "recreate the classical cooking that derived from Renaissance Italy." Beef Saltimbocca and Chicken Campisano became favorites. "We adapted the name saltimbocca to a filet that we cut and stuffed with prosciutto and provolone, grilled and topped with sautéed mushrooms," says Paul Grisanti.

Newspaper critic Robin Garr praised Ferd Grisanti's food. In 1986, he awarded three stars, enjoying the "savory, garlicky fettuccine with white clam sauce" and writing that the "seven-course Tastes of Tuscany banquet" was a "food phantasmagoria." In 1990, Garr went even further, awarding four stars while raving about the saltimbocca, "a creamy, delectable version" of pesto Genovese and house-made gelato that "made a rousing finish to an excellent meal." Paul Grisanti remembers the four-star review and the gelato machine that helped make it happen: "Nancy Shepherd [of Cafe Metro and Uptown Cafe] came to our restaurant, and she said 'Goddamn Paul, what you need here is gelato! I have a gelato machine my husband bought that I have no frickin' use for.' (She did not use the word 'frickin.')…We started making gelato, and that's when we got our first four-star rating."

Ferd Grisanti died in 1993, two years after the fancy downtown restaurant he had sold his share in twenty years earlier had closed. "Dad worked almost to the day he died," says Paul Grisanti. Suffering from Parkinson's, "he was shuffling and his hands were shaky, but he would go from table to table and talk to everybody." The brothers continued to run the restaurant without him, but by 2002, Paul began to explore a career in real estate. In 2007, the J-town Grisanti brothers sold their restaurant. The new owner, a first-time operator facing a difficult economy with little restaurant experience, couldn't keep the restaurant running, and in 2008, the Grisanti landlords shut it down.

Today, Loui Loui's Authentic Detroit Style Pizza operates in the space that was once Ferd Grisanti's, but the old restaurant has yet to disappear. Stop in on the second Tuesday of just about any month and Vince Grisanti shoud be there, hosting a special "Ferd Night." He may cook veal alla panna,

Chapter 32

JAY'S

Fighting Prejudice with Family-Style Food

Louisville's West End Russell neighborhood has not always struggled. Roughly bounded by Ninth Street to the east, Market Street to the north, Broadway to the south and Thirty-second Street to the west, the area first began to expand after the Civil War, as prominent German businessmen followed Louisville's streetcar lines westward in the 1880s. The neighborhood, once a mix of stately mansions, working-class houses and businesses, became the home of many prominent African Americans. Up through the Second World War, Russell's section of Walnut Street (now Muhammad Ali Boulevard) was busy with black entrepreneurs, big-name entertainers and plenty of traffic. But by the 1960s, Russell's star had faded. Integration opened the door for middle-class blacks to move to other areas while urban renewal programs began to level entire blocks, leaving the neighborhood named for noted educator Harvey Clarence Russell Sr. littered with vacant lots and abandoned buildings. Despite the challenges of a changing neighborhood, Frank Foster created a cafeteria that became a center of the Russell community—and today stands ready to help the neighborhood grow again.

Foster's first experience in the food business came in the late 1960s, when he managed a chicken shack for Gilbert Hardwick. Foster and Hardwick parted ways, and Foster took up selling baked goods. By 1974, Foster had decided he wanted to give the restaurant business a second go. He rented the shack back from Hardwick and came up with the name "Jay's" because he thought it was easy to remember. As 1980s factory closings meant fewer workers in West Louisville, Foster, along with his wife, Barbara, and brother Norman, struggled at 504 South Eighteenth Street. But they persevered, keeping their cafeteria lines full of "an appetizing line of Kentucky cooking" at amazingly low prices, and the restaurant began to pack in the people. A 1991 *Courier-Journal* article described the scene:

> *At noon two things greet you at the door of Jay's Cafeteria: the tantalizing aroma of good home cooking and a long line of hungry customers. Few people turn away. Most suffer through the cafeteria line to reach a hearty helping of Jay's standards—fried chicken, smothered pork chops, pig's feet, ham hocks, fried buffalo fish, barbecue ribs, boiled okra, green beans, stewed apples or baked macaroni-and-cheese. And more. After choosing among the daily menu's seven meat dishes and seven to 10 vegetables, your eyes are tested by such tempting desserts as apple and peach cobbler, pound cake and banana pudding. At the end of the line are the tossed salads, looking untouched and unloved—more like garnishes for the other, more popular dishes.*

The author observed that "overeating…[was] in vogue at Jay's," where patrons could enjoy "a hefty meal for about $5."

Foster's food helped him combat the impression of white Louisvillians that Jay's was on the wrong side of town. Restaurant guides noted "two well-lit…off-street parking lots," and the Fosters worked hard to keep Jay's "a clean place, [with] good friendly service at moderate prices." Especially at lunch, "professionals in pinstripes, laborers, ministers, retirees—black and white" all walked through with their cafeteria trays. Foster told the *Courier-Journal* Jay's was "one of the few places where the so-called welfare recipient and the bank president ever line up behind each other."

From chitlins to cobbler, none of Jay's recipes was written down and nobody called it "soul food." Foster believed "soul food" implied dishes enjoyed by only black people, insisting instead that Jay's was "a family restaurant" with "something for everyone."

Jay's became so popular that Foster expanded the business, creating a fourteen-thousand-square-foot building just west of his initial location. Jay's, then crowned by a smiling African American chef icon, moved its entrance to Muhammad Ali Boulevard and kept on serving what Foster described as family-style food. Called a "testament to entrepreneurship" by Louisville's mayor and business leaders, Jay's expanded space was described by Foster as "the grand palace of the West End."

Jay's diners. *Courtesy of John Nation.*

Larger spaces meant larger crowds, who kept lining up for fried chicken, macaroni and cheese ("sunshine yellow with lots of real cheese"), greens, smothered pork chops and "homemade biscuits and cornbread and peach cobbler with lots of sugar baked into the juicy crust" along with lots of other desserts. In 2004, Jay's hosted a call center for the Obama campaign, and the restaurant happily entertained Michelle Obama, who came to thank supporters who came "from Metro Louisville and across the country."

But the financial troubles of the early 2000s and the demise of the Philip Morris cigarette factory on Broadway forced the Fosters to close. Jay's was sold to a church ministry, which reopened the restaurant as an "all-you-can-eat" buffet in 2005. It didn't last long. The Fosters' food can still be found at Franco's Restaurant & Catering in Shively, where son Dominic serves up "smothered pork chops, collard greens, fried chicken, fried catfish and fruit cobbler," and Frank can be found in the dining room almost every day.

Frank Foster's "grand palace of the West End" is not yet done. A local nonprofit has broken ground on a "food incubator" at the former Jay's, "dedicated to fostering early-stage catering, retail and wholesale food businesses." So, while the Fosters may no longer call Jay's home, their restaurant could one day become another "testament to entrepreneurship."

Chapter 33

THE FIG TREE

Fighting a Ghost, Forging the Mettle of "Louisville's Alice Waters"

The Fig Tree wasn't the first restaurant to operate in the Weissinger-Gaulbert apartment building. A 1912 advertisement touting "the only modern, up-to-date Apartment Building in Louisville" mentions a "restaurant in connection," and other establishments undoubtedly took advantage of the corner of Third Street and Broadway before the Fig Tree arrived in 1974. The owners, including Stanley Pekarsky, had built a successful restaurant by the same name in Lexington and decided it was time to move up to Louisville.

Pekarsky, who had been chef at the original Fig Tree, had applicants for the head chef position at the Louisville restaurant "audition" by preparing a dinner for him. He told an interviewer in 1975 that he "couldn't choose a chef by talking [because he didn't] know the right questions to ask." One audition menu began with deep-fried Gruyère cheese (something the young applicant chef called "pohana sir") and a spinach soufflé. The main course was beef marinated in whiskey with souffléd potatoes. There was also spinach salad and chocolate mousse. Pekarsky found it "elegantly served" and appreciated how the chef "paid attention to the details." He hired that chef, Katherine Nash, a twenty-one-year-old Prospect native who had returned from catering and restaurant work in Washington, D.C.

While the restaurant became an almost immediate hit, the Fig Tree almost made Katherine Nash, now better known as Kathy Cary, quit the restaurant business. If that had happened, Louisville might not have the restaurant

Weissinger-Gaulbert Building, site of Fig Tree. *Michelle Turner.*

reputation it holds today. Cary, who legendary restaurateur Bim Deitrich calls "our Alice Waters" for her pioneering work sparking Louisville's farm-to-table movement and who has been nominated for several James Beard and other culinary awards, thought her first head chef position would be where she could have "the freedom to do my recipes, to interpret my knowledge into cuisine." Little did she know what "an awful year it would be."

A 1975 newspaper article describes one of the young chef's days at the restaurant, which began at 9:00 a.m. and was far from over as dinner service began around 6:30 p.m.:

> *Although she declines to wear the traditional chef's hat, a "toque blanche,"— "It's not me," she said—Miss Nash wore several hats that day. She prepared some dishes, supervised others' food preparations, checked deliveries of food to the restaurant and often carried the boxes to the freezer, interviewed a job applicant, swept the floor and washed by hand dozens of dirty dishes after the dishwasher broke down during lunch. The dinner that was ready to be served that night had been planned the week before when she wrote the menu.*

"Stan Pekarsky's idea was to change the lunch menu every day to 'keep it interesting,'" Cary says. "We'd change the dinner menu every two weeks, and you'd have a special every day. It was hard." Cary fought to win the respect of not only her mostly much older employees but also grizzled vendors at places like the Fulton Fish Market. She dragged drunk employees out of strip clubs and cooked dishes such as caviar mousse, chicken rosemary, *gâteau aux amandes* and Linzer torte. After an eighteen- or nineteen-hour day, she would go to her apartment above the restaurant and get ready for the next round.

"I cried a lot," Cary says. "If I saw anyone I knew come in the front door, I would burst into tears. I'd walk across the room just crying." Cary recalls that, during her tenure, the owners "would sit upstairs and basically count their money," putting their profits first and leaving her to explain to the staff why their paychecks were late. "I had somebody threaten me with a butcher knife," remembers Cary. After about six months, Cary says, "it dawned on me that nothing was getting better, that it was getting worse." By 1976, she'd had enough and left the Fig Tree to work for Stewart's, becoming a fashion director.

The Fig Tree kept going. In 1977, Carte Blanche gave the Fig Tree one of only fifty-five "Epicurean Awards," saluting "a remarkable restaurant and its guiding genius Stan Pekarsky." In 1978, United Airlines' in-flight magazine selected the restaurant for its "Excellence in Dining" award, calling the Fig Tree "a great American restaurant." Pekarsky's yen to "keep it interesting" led to publishing menus a month in advance, with a different selection of courses every day. Dishes included Strawberry Soup, Veal Schnitzel Maria Teresa, Flank Steak Stuffed with Oysters, Green Bean Nicoise and much, much more. The restaurant also offered take-away service, promising a constantly rotating array of soups, sandwiches and other items.

But by 1980, the Fig Tree was closed. The new majority owner, Phyllis Heideman, told the *Courier-Journal* that Pekarsky "departed in 1979" with "business debts." What really irritated Heideman were "recent unfavorable reviews" in both the Bingham newspapers, which she claimed "destroyed any remaining hope of the restaurant to survive." Heideman complained that although "operations had improved greatly in recent months," reviews in the newspapers "continued to unfairly compare it with its performance under past management." Bitter about the refusal of Louisville to give the Fig Tree a second chance, Heideman observed, "You can't fight a ghost."

Kathy Nash Cary, however, had a different idea. Her job as fashion director at Stewart's meant she "got to go to New York a lot and eat in nice places," which helped widen her culinary horizons. The position also helped her catering business, which she restarted with a friend and fellow Stewart's employee. Eventually, Cary went into business for herself as La Peche Catering and then opened Lilly's Restaurant. She's still there, leading a kitchen through the lessons learned at the Fig Tree: "After that experience, I knew I would never again work in a place I didn't own, and I would never manage it as poorly as the owners of the Fig Tree." While the ghosts of the restaurant at Third and Broadway may still be in Louisville, their spirit may be helping to drive Kathy Cary to continue adding to Louisville's fine restaurant reputation.

Chapter 34
SIXTH AVENUE
Setting Standards, Seeding Chefs

In 1981, the Grisanti family was feeling fine. Casa Grisanti, the family's flagship restaurant, had been lauded by the *New York Times*, *Esquire* and other national publications. Mamma Grisanti, their franchise-ready family-style Italian place in Dupont, was doing good business. Don Grisanti had resigned as president of Grisanti Inc., leaving to study art history. Instead of school, brother Michael Grisanti and partner Vincenzo Gabriele decided to start another restaurant in a building across the street from the spanking-new Kentucky Center for the Arts.

Built in the mid-1850s, the building at Sixth and Main Streets originally held businesses, including a clothing store. In 1880, Louis Seelbach opened a bar, restaurant and billiard room and, by 1886, had turned it into a hotel. In 1900, Louis and his brother remodeled the structure to include a central stained-glass light well. By the late 1970s, the building had been boarded up, its only patrons vagrants and vandals. But spurred by the arts center and other downtown renovation efforts, the building was restored and beautifully adapted for modern use, including space for a ground-floor restaurant, taking advantage of the large open central atrium. That space became Sixth Avenue, Restaurant of the Americas.

In a 1981 article written right before the restaurant was to open, Grisanti and Gabriele said they wanted to do with "seafood—cooked to 'Classic American' recipes" what they "did with Northern Italian cuisine at Casa." They pointed out the new stainless steel grill, specially designed to cook fish that would "never be touched by electric or gas heat" but instead gain flavor from "hard to find"

Site of Sixth Avenue, 600 West Main Street. *Michelle Turner.*

mesquite charcoal "imported from Mexico." The restaurant's menu announced that "only recently has an American cuisine come to be recognized," calling it "a cuisine that is historically evolved from our country's regional and ethnic diversity." Recalling the restaurant in 2012 for *Louisville Magazine*, Jack Welch described "a more youthful West Main alternative to East Liberty Street's Casa Grisanti" even though, at first, coats and ties were required.

In 1982, the Grisantis sponsored the "First Symposium on American Cuisine," which the *Chicago Tribune* called "one-of-a-kind." It drew 131 restaurateurs, food service people, critics, editors, cooking school owners and others, "who explored and celebrated the rising of a national cuisine." Attendees included New York restaurant critic Gael Greene, California winemaker Robert Mondavi and New Orleans chef Paul Prudhomme, as well as local chefs such as Bim Deitrich. The *Washington Post*'s Phyllis Richman wrote, "Nobody could agree on what exactly to call…[the style, and e]ven weaker was the consensus on how to define it, beyond Americans cooking with American ingredients…But the newest, most pervasive theme of New American Cookery is the search for the best of American ingredients, local when possible and always fresh."

Beyond the symposium, Sixth Avenue quickly gained notice for its elegant, spacious interior and its seafood, as well as what a 1983 restaurant guide referred to as "the largest selection of American wines in Kentucky." The Grisantis had hired Frank Yang out of New York's Playboy Club to be executive chef. Yang quickly staffed his kitchen with talent, including chef Mark Stevens, then fresh out of cooking school, and a young man returning to Louisville from Texas named Dean Corbett. Stevens described Sixth Avenue's American Cuisine as "things our grandmothers brought to this country and adapted to the regions in which they settled." The menu featured dishes such as Kitty Hawk Spiced Shrimp, Pan Fried Catfish (in orange butter with candied orange zest) and "Owensboro" boned, barbecued chicken. In the *New York Times*, Regina Schrambling approved of Sixth Avenue's "1980's touch to the Hot Brown," which used Wolferman's English muffins and Kentucky country ham. A 1986 three-star review in the *Scene* raved about "chunky New England chowder," desserts and "competent and cheerful" service.

But something, perhaps success itself, ended what had been a key part of downtown's resurgent restaurant scene. Grisanti, Inc. was sold to a Canadian holding company. Jack Welch wrote that "something happened internally, and it swung towards a Southwest-influenced menu," which is evidenced by a bizarre tableau that contains a rifle-holding, serape-and-sombrero-clad mannequin shown in a photograph included in this volume. The dress code went from well-dressed to whatever. By late 1989, Robin Garr was writing Sixth Avenue's obituary, saying the news of "the demise of Sixth Avenue, which had been not merely one of downtown's most pleasant restaurants but a national leader in American cuisine before it began slipping in its final months—has to rank as the year's worst restaurant news."

What was once the site of an exploration of American foodstuffs is now home to an association of lawyers. Frank Yang left to start Ditto's, and Mark Stevens has his own deli, Stevens & Stevens, in an adjoining space. Dean Corbett became one of Louisville's leading chefs, starting and financing several well-respected restaurants. Countless other Sixth Avenue alumni are cooking, hosting, serving and working around Louisville. Mesquite grilling may no longer be a novelty, but the influence Sixth Avenue's "New American Cuisine" is still very much a part of Louisville.

Chapter 35

CAFE METRO

Making Bardstown Road "Restaurant Row"

In the late 1970s, Louisville's best postgame party was in Seneca Gardens. Nancy Shepherd, an English and humanities teacher at Seneca High School, lived on Broadmeade with her husband, David, and daughter, Kelly. Renting the house next door were some culinary students, including a young man named Ed Garber. "Ed was interested in food, and David was interested in food," says Nancy Shepherd. "Every Sunday we would play volleyball, and afterward Ed Garber would go in his kitchen, and David Shepherd would go in his, and they would try to out-cook one another. So it was a fun, fun day to be on Broadmeade." That group of friends, brought together for Sunday volleyball, helped create a "food first" attitude toward fine dining that has become a significant part of Louisville's restaurant culture. And the Shepherds started the city's first "Restaurant Row."

Nancy Shepherd describes her husband as "a very mercurial person," adding, "That's a nice way of saying bipolar." Dissatisfied with his degree in business and accounting, David Shepherd decided to go to Europe. "He went over on a program where you could study architecture in Florence," says Nancy, came back and "was like 'Man, I just want to do food.'" Ed Garber went first, opening 610 Magnolia after David Shepherd helped remodel the building, which Nancy describes as "a piece of shit ready to fall down." But once his friend got going, David "decided if Ed could do it, he could do it." So the Shepherds found a partner and began to fulfill David's vision of a restaurant where he could cook and Nancy could host.

They leased the former Mario's Pizza on Bardstown Road, and Cafe Metro became a reality.

"A neighborhood café is what David wanted to do," Nancy recalls. "He just wanted to make a living working with food." But the initial almost round-the-clock hours didn't last. "We were so incredibly stupid about what it was to do a business, especially a restaurant," Shepherd remembers. "We were open for breakfast, lunch and dinner for only one week." The business partner backed out after that disastrous week, and Cafe Metro closed "to work out some problems." The Shepherds abandoned the idea of breakfast, cashed in Nancy's retirement account, borrowed from David's parents and began to refocus on their core idea.

"Our concept was that fine dining should be for everybody, and there wasn't anyplace in town that was like that" except Garber's Old Louisville restaurant in its earliest days, remembers Nancy Shepherd. In 1981, when Cafe Metro opened, the downtown Grisantis were setting the standard for fine dining in Louisville, insisting on coats and ties at both their restaurants. The Shepherds thought dining could be different: "We thought you should be able to have the finest experience and it wouldn't be cob-up-the-ass." Instead, it would be "accessible."

This idea, crystallized in Cafe Metro when it reopened a few weeks later, was almost immediately well received. Reviewers noted that, despite the "white linens and fresh flowers," the restaurant felt "casual," due in part to Nancy Shepherd's "pleasant personality." (Shepherd recalls that her husband deemed her "the best door whore in the business.") One writer called Cafe Metro's steak au poivre "the best…[he'd] had in a place that was not…[his] own home," and raved about his Empress Carlotta Torte—"rich

Cafe Metro mural. *Stephen Hacker.*

layers of chocolate and buttercream flavored with Kahlua and sumptuously festooned with toasted almond slivers and powdered sugar." In 1982, critic Ken Neuhauser wrote that Cafe Metro sent "thrills up and down…[his] taste buds," as the "fresh flowers, plants and the whirring sound of the cappuccino machine in the background combine[d] to present a casually chic ambience." Diners were blown away by baked Brie with almonds and sliced apples, salmon filet with dill and lemon butter, "Mexican egg rolls filled with green chilis, Monterey Jack cheese" and more. The restaurant kept gaining popularity, and Louisvillians began rethinking their perceptions of Bardstown Road.

In 1984, the president of "Bardstown Road Tomorrow" remembered when people "didn't like to go down Bardstown Road because it was dirty, it was hard to find parking, and businesses were kind of grungy looking." But by the dawn of Ronald Reagan's second term, the street was changing—though the parking situation wasn't getting much better. And while the Shepherds gave credit to the Bristol's 1977 opening as the "obvious leader" in a new wave of restaurants, Cafe Metro was constantly mentioned as a key part of the revival. As other restaurants began to occupy the former hardware stores, bars and beauty shops, Cafe Metro added additional dining space. By 1986, David Shepherd had convinced Nancy that they could operate another restaurant, though Nancy insisted it be "close enough to Cafe Metro that…[she] could take care of it." The Shepherds bought what had been the Tim Tam Two bar just across Duker Street ("cheap liquor, but you might have something crawl up you," recalls Nancy Shepherd) and began converting it into the Uptown Cafe. As the Shepherds were planning a possible third restaurant, a series of tragedies began.

Working at Cafe Metro one night in 1986, Nancy Shepherd "felt like someone had put a piece of concrete" on her head and had "beaten it with a sledgehammer." It was a cerebral hemorrhage. Doctors said Nancy was lucky to survive, and she needed therapy to relearn how to read and write. Not long afterward, a smoldering cigarette ignited a couch, seriously damaging the Shepherds' home. David and Nancy separated, and in 1988, while still trying to assess what they could do with their property, David drove his car into a tree and was killed. Instead of shuttering, Cafe Metro kept cooking, closing only on the day of David's memorial service and even then hosting out-of-town mourners to talk and remember. "We don't like this stuff at all," Nancy Shepherd told a reporter, "but we're just fine. This is not a sad story."

After David's death, Nancy Shepherd became even more the heart and soul of Cafe Metro, spending much of her time looking after her customers and staff. *Louisville Magazine*'s Jack Welch called Nancy Cafe Metro's "sprightliest touch of all"—positioned, as she almost always was, "at the end of the restaurant's small bar, two steps from the menu rack and another half-dozen from the front door." To critic Susan Reigler, Nancy's warm greetings were almost as good as the food: "Her jubilant cries of 'Hello, sweetie!' or 'Welcome, my dear!' echo like a horn signaling beagles at a hunt. It's the only 'noisy' aspect of the otherwise subdued restaurant, and her genuine happiness at seeing patrons—regulars or newcomers—always makes me smile."

Nancy was always good-naturedly egalitarian, proudly relating her reaction to "some in-for-the-weekend big wheel who would try to finagle a table by announcing, 'Do you know who I am?'" Shepherd says that she would secretly think, "Yes. You're an asshole" but instead simply replied, "No, sir, I do not. But I do know who these [other waiting] people are, and I see them every week." That was when Cafe Metro wasn't taking reservations, which Shepherd began to do when "we had enough competition that people wouldn't stand around and wait anymore."

Nancy thought it was "psychologically good for the staff, especially for the ones in the kitchen who spend their time with fire in their faces," to feel that she was "on the line with them." Over the years, a number of chefs, including Dennis Schroeder, Eric Sinnott, David Barnes and Michael Crouch, added their touches to the kitchen. But, even long after Nancy quit writing the menu by hand, the Jaegerschnitzel ("breaded veal scallopini in a brown cream sauce with pepper and mushrooms") that a German friend had taught David Shepherd to make was almost always there. Nancy's favorites included the escargots, which she thought were "the best in town," and the chicken with smoked goose. "We had to order [the goose] from New York. It was expensive as shit," she said. But what most people remember are the incredible desserts, baked by Jenna Mooser and other pastry chefs, including Gateau Ganache ("crunchy walnut meringue layered with Chantilly cream") and the Concorde ("alternating layers of chocolate mousse and chocolate meringue topped with curls of chocolate meringue").

Cafe Metro kept making people happy long after Bardstown Road became filled with restaurants of all varieties. But as the economy struggled in the early twenty-first century, so did the idea of fine dining, and in 2009, Cafe Metro closed after twenty-eight years. "We'd always been a special occasion restaurant," says Nancy Shepherd, "but when the economy started dipping, people started going to the Uptown. The quality was the same, you just weren't going to get the fancy ingredients. I put a whole bunch of money in [Cafe Metro] trying to keep it open. I just didn't want to give it up. I'm enormously proud of the Uptown, but it isn't my heart like the Metro was."

Some signature Cafe Metro dishes were transported across the street to the Uptown, but Nancy Shepherd did not go with them. When she asked her daughter if she could help there, Shepherd says Kelly responded, "Mother, your restaurant's gone. You'd be in the way." Nancy laughingly recalls that her response was, "Fuck you, bitch," but let her daughter have her way.

Blue jeans and formal wear now mingle freely at most of Louisville's "fine dining" restaurants. Nancy Shepherd still appears at the Uptown regularly but only to enjoy herself and perhaps peek across the street at the mural on the wall of what is now Wild Ginger Sushi. The scene depicts her favorite artwork, admiring passersby and portraits of her idols, Ernest Hemingway and Julia Child, the latter of which is often mistaken for Nancy herself. ("That is not I. It is Julia.") Traffic and parking may still be problems on Bardstown Road, but finding a good restaurant isn't one any longer—thanks, in large part, to a vision of casual enjoyment and a kind, intelligent and strong-willed woman who lent Cafe Metro her incredible personality and charm.

Chapter 36

AFRO-GERMAN TEA ROOM

Rescuing a Parish with a Restaurant

There are many signs of Louisville's significant German heritage, but the church of St. Martin of Tours may be the most flamboyant. The parish began in 1853, at a time when native Germans and their descendants made up over a third of Louisville's population. When some ugly locals became unhappy about that, the new church building came in handy. On "Bloody Monday," August 6, 1855, as the anti-immigrant American Party rioted, looted and murdered throughout Louisville, a mob descended on St. Martin's. A cannon was positioned in front of the church, as rioters accused the Catholics of hiding arms and explosives. Fortunately, Mayor John Barbee, the supposed hero of the "Know-Nothings," stood in front of the church door, and the cannon was removed.

Saved from destruction, St. Martin's continued to expand. Some Ursuline Sisters from Bavaria established a school. The church was enlarged to the shape of a cross. In 1861, as the Civil War began, a great organ arrived from Germany. After the war, the church had several more additions, including German-made stained-glass windows and Stations of the Cross. In 1901, St. Martin's acquired full skeletal relics of the early Christian martyrs Magnus and Bonosa, housing them in glass reliquaries in the ornately decorated interior.

Anti-German sentiment came to Louisville again during World War I, and the Phoenix Hill parish began to lose members. Germany's aggression in the Second World War didn't help the country's reputation a generation later, and postwar suburban expansion meant St. Martin's continued to slide.

By the 1970s, there were only about thirty parishioners, and the neighborhood population had become small, poor and mostly African American. People were beginning to speak of St. Martin of Tours as something that had passed. Then Vernon Robertson came, and the church began to move in another direction—through the kitchen.

Father Robertson began his career as a priest in the West End. He helped found Louisville's Urban Montessori Schools and the city's first residence for people with AIDS. Years before he came to St. Martin's, during a visit to Rome, Robertson saw some women running a restaurant called Living Water, which served French cuisine to raise money for missionary work. As

St. Martin of Tours. *Michelle Turner.*

the original priest's dining room at St. Martin's was available, the new priest decided he could do the same thing.

The Afro-German Tea Room opened in April 1984. A week later, Robertson told the *Courier-Journal* the restaurant "had as much as we can handle." Located in the church rectory, the tearoom served lunch, dinner and Sunday brunch for its seven tables. It used mostly volunteer cooks and servers, and profits supported the parish's Montessori school.

Despite the lack of paid chefs and the odd entry through the kitchen, critics and customers loved the tearoom, calling it "a little romantic and extremely eclectic." Robertson and his sister, DeeDee Stokes, decided on a "continental-style menu combining to-order European salutes with many American favorites," defying many people's expectations. "Some people expect[ed] a covered-dish supper," Robertson told a reporter, noting the name also made some think they'd "find bratwurst and potato salad, or chitlins and sauerkraut." Instead, crusty Italian bread was baked every day. Lunch menus included artichoke and provolone and homemade pimiento cheese sandwiches, soups, salads and desserts. Dinner might feature Baltimore crab cakes or fresh artichoke bottoms stuffed with shrimp. A special dinner called "Homage to James Beard" included yellow-tailed snapper, barbecue spare ribs, Block Island swordfish, New York cheesecake and strawberry shortcake.

Food was presented on colorful, handmade Italian dishes. The coral-peach-olive interior featured local artwork. The Afro-German expanded from the main dining room into another room upstairs and what *Louisville Magazine*'s Agnes Crume described as "an adjoining screened porch that…[held] a table for six with a graceful candelabra and a view of the environs." Father Robertson seemed to enjoy the restaurant business and often toured the dining rooms, shaking hands and introducing himself to customers. It was reported that, when asked by a priest how they liked the food, many Catholic Louisvillians "found it difficult to lie."

Robertson's innovative fundraising idea not only helped the Montessori school but also helped keep St. Martin's active and operating. By 1995, the parish had grown confident enough that it decided it needed the rectory for other uses, and the Afro-German Tea Room was closed. Martin of Tours, Father Vernon Robertson once told a reporter, was known as the patron saint of restaurants. But for the parish named for the noble French knight, the real restaurant patron saint was a humble priest, helped by his devoted sister.

Apple Crisp

Adapted from the Afro-German Tea Room's recipe published in the *Courier-Journal*. Serves 4–6.

Topping:
¾ cup flour
1 stick (8 tablespoons) unsalted butter, cut into small pieces
¼ cup white sugar
¼ cup brown sugar
pinch salt
¾ cup coarsely chopped walnuts or pecans

Filling:
4 or 5 tart apples
¼ cup brown sugar
¼ cup white sugar
pinch salt
1 tablespoon dark rum
½ teaspoon vanilla
½ teaspoon nutmeg
1 teaspoon cinnamon

Heat oven to 350 degrees. Generously butter an 8- or 9-inch casserole dish.

In a medium bowl, mix together flour and butter with a pastry blender or fingers as if making a pie crust or biscuits. Add remaining topping ingredients and toss to combine.

Peel, core and thinly slice apples. Place in a large bowl and toss with remaining filling ingredients.

Pour apple filling into prepared casserole dish. Sprinkle topping over. Bake for about 45 minutes, until topping is browned and apples are bubbling.

Serve with sweetened whipped cream.

Chapter 37
DE LA TORRE'S

Studiously Spanish for Over Two Decades

Maggie de la Torre married young, spending the first part of her adult life as the wife of an oil executive, traveling the world as a mother. After a divorce, Maggie took her children to Madrid, where she had learned Spanish and fallen in love with the city several years earlier. She bought a stake in a local restaurant and began learning the business. She met and fell in love with a Madrileño chef named Miguel. Married in Gibraltar in 1987, they decided to return to America to open a restaurant together. "I wanted to come somewhere…familiar," Maggie de la Torre told a *Business First* reporter, saying she chose Louisville because she knew the city and thought it would be "a great place to raise children."

In 1988, the couple opened De la Torre's on Bardstown Road. Cool tiles, soft lights and the knowledgeable stewardship of Maggie were among its rustic, old-world charms. "We decided we were going to have our own space of Spain in this city," said Miguel de la Torre. Louisville was introduced to Castilian-style roast lamb, Spanish cheeses and paella and fell in love. Quietly (the restaurant did not advertise) and confidently, De la Torre's kept the Spanish flavor going. Flamenco dancing and the songs of *cantautores* were often seen and heard as people kept discovering and enjoying what was to Louisville an entirely new cuisine.

In 2004, the de la Torres celebrated their restaurant's fifteenth anniversary by opening a tapas bar called La Bodega next door. Unlike De la Torre's, which tended toward a quiet and dignified atmosphere, La Bodega offered tapas, late-night dining and a full bar with specialty cocktails. Though a fire above La Bodega in 2008 temporarily shuttered both places, the sibling restaurants kept satisfying their customers. The same year, critic Robin Garr praised Miguel's "wake-up-your-taste-buds spicy salsa brava," roasted lamb "cooked until it was falling-apart tender and served in its natural juices in a handsome

De la Torre's sign. *Michelle Turner.*

brown ceramic crock" and "three perfect scallops," which were "sweet and just cooked through, a frog-hair past sushi style."

De la Torre's was still popular as it approached another milestone, its twenty-fifth anniversary. Instead of opening another restaurant, the de la Torres decided to retire. Maggie told a reporter that, with a new grandchild and children living on separate coasts, she and Miguel wanted more time to travel and spend time with family. She told another that it was "really a bittersweet feeling, but it's time for it to end…Let's be honest, you don't want to stay at the dance too long." The building was sold to another couple, who opened a restaurant featuring small plates—an idea that, unlike when the de la Torres opened their restaurant, Louisville is now quite familiar with.

Chapter 38

TIMOTHY'S

Louisville's White Chili "Inventors"

Tim Barnes would likely have preferred to be remembered more for hit Broadway shows than Great Northern beans. His friend and former partner, Bim Deitrich, remembers that Barnes, who came from a family of western Kentucky bankers, "loved music. He produced a couple of Broadway shows, though none of them ever went anywhere." But, Deitrich added, "he liked the restaurant business, too." Indeed, his *Courier-Journal* obituary noted that Barnes once said running a restaurant was "a lot like theater." Barnes "produced and created; he had his props; the menu was his script; and the characters were his food. Then, he said, 'You either got a good review or a bad review.'" While his theater work may not have gone far, Barnes's restaurants are still fondly remembered by many Louisvillians, especially his last effort, Timothy's—where, locals believe, Barnes invented the dish known as white chili.

Barnes, who was born in Lexington, grew up in Owensboro. He spent some time as a vice-president of the Beaver Dam Deposit Bank and also worked as a buyer for Kaufman's Department Store in Louisville. While attending graduate school in Atlanta, Barnes got into the restaurant and bar business.

Barnes sold his interests in the Georgia ventures and headed for Louisville in the early 1970s. He first took over the vacant restaurant space in Old Louisville's Mayflower Hotel on West Ormsby Avenue, calling his restaurant J. Timothy's. Barnes told the *Courier-Journal* in 1974 that he "wanted a people place where I could do my thing with food, my menu, my recipes." He said he wanted his restaurant "to be comfortable, not elegant." Barnes said, "The atmosphere I like was the other Saturday night when hippies in their denims sat in one corner and Paul King and his party from the orchestra concert were in another." Barnes's "special touches" at J. Timothy's included "telephones that…[could] be plugged in at each table and a salad cart with crocks of homemade dressings that's wheeled to tables." However, downtown business was declining, and by 1975, dinnertime business was so slow that Barnes, who had already decided to close his restaurant before the year's end, complained about rumors that he had already closed, adding, "I'd hate to see business get any slower the closer we get to closing night."

The declining downtown business didn't deter Barnes from Louisville restaurants, however. A few years later, he purchased Myra's, a restaurant "run by a jolly woman of the same name whose pies were legend" on Grinstead Drive next to Burger's Market. Barnes painted the ceiling black and the walls clay red and, according to some reports, called it "Formerly Myra's." But Deitrich, who became Barnes's partner in 1982, insists Barnes called it "Formally Myra's," which Deitrich wanted changed as soon as he became involved. "The name was pretentious," Deitrich says, "it confused people, and some thought they were actually supposed to wear a tuxedo." Whatever they called it, Louisvillians seemed to enjoy what some called "a curious combination of the informal and formal," with Barnes telling *Louisville Magazine* in 1983, "We get people in tuxedos eating hamburgers and people in cut-offs eating filets."

Both Deitrich and Barnes became interested in other projects, especially after the Burgers, who owned the property, started to think about expanding their grocery. Deitrich went on to establish his eponymous restaurant in the old Crescent Theater. Barnes decided to go on Broadway, and in 1988, he opened Timothy's on the corner of Broadway and Logan. The restaurant was a hit. *Louisville Magazine*'s Mary Welp recalled "the welcoming awnings, the dark wood of the bar…the down-home front room" and a second Art Deco–styled area "that made you feel like an escapee from *To Have and To Have Not*." There were red walls, leopard-skin carpeting and an eclectic menu, which included the dish Timothy's became famous for, white chili.

Described as a "delicious" mixture of white beans and chicken breast "flavored with green chilies, cumin, a pinch of cloves and cayenne pepper and topped with a white Monterey Jack cheese and sour cream," white chili was an immediate sensation. Patrons besieged Barnes and his chef, James Aydlett, for the recipe, which later appeared in *Bon Appétit Magazine*. Many

Timothy's white chili. *Courtesy of John Nation.*

bemoaned the fact that, unlike the canny Kerns and their Derby-Pie®, the restaurant never applied for a trademark. One origin story was that Aydlett came up with white chili after traveling in the Southwest. Another had Barnes saying he had "made it up, kind of as a prank he pulled on some of his friends." But the truth, it turns out, was much simpler.

In 1992, after both Aydlett and Barnes had died, an article in the *Courier-Journal* reported that Stephen Lee, owner of the Cookbook Cottage on Bardstown Road, remembered Barnes telling him he was thinking of opening a restaurant and asking Lee to pick out "some hot new cookbooks." One Lee selected was *Beyond Parsley*, a 1984 compilation of recipes from the Junior League of Kansas City. That cookbook had a recipe for "white chili," made with white beans and chicken instead of red beans and beef. While Lee acknowledged that Barnes read the cookbook, he credited his friend with improving the dish. "After I tasted his, I made the white chili from the cookbook," Lee told a reporter, saying that Barnes's version "had more zest."

After Barnes's death in 1990, his sister and, after her, other operators continued Timothy's for a while, but the restaurant was never the same. The historic building at Broadway and Logan has been razed. The curtain may have rung down on J. Timothy Barnes, but his white chili recipe remains. It joins other names on the Derby City marquee such as Hot Brown, Benedictine, rolled oysters and the cheeseburger—the last of which, like white chili, Louisvillians will continue to claim as their own, despite all evidence to the contrary.

Chapter 39

DEITRICH'S

Freemasonry Fosters Frankfort Avenue's Restaurant Row

Today, the Frankfort Avenue Business Association proudly says there are "more than 30 locally owned restaurants located along a 2.5 mile stretch" connecting the St. Matthews, Crescent Hill and Clifton neighborhoods. Highly rated restaurants create (as the boosters say) "a culinary hub that boasts *al fresco* dining, many options for international cuisine, and unique flavors of the city." But if it weren't for the Free and Accepted Masons and a man named "Bim," it may never have happened.

The tan brick Classical Revival building dates back to 1927, or A.L. 5927 (as F.&A.M. Lodge 820 inscribed on the cornerstone). The actual temple was on the top floors, as the crafty Masons built the structure with revenue in mind, including a real estate office, a dry cleaner and a 525-seat theater. Now part of the Crescent Hill Historic District, the Crescent Theater was first a family movie house with occasional vaudeville and magic acts and then an "art house" showing entertainment such as the Italian crime drama *Indagine su un Cittadino al di Sopra di Ogni Sospetto*, as seen there by a young man by the name of Ralph Edward "Bim" Deitrich when visiting Louisville in 1971. By the mid-1980s, the Crescent had deteriorated into an X-rated venue, and Bim Deitrich had become one of the rising stars of the city's restaurant scene.

Deitrich, who grew up working in his parents' hotel business in Maine, made friends from Louisville while attending Washington and Lee University. In 1972, he helped open the Hearthstone Tavern downtown with a fellow Washington and Lee alum, Doug Gossman, and owner Paul O'Brien. "It was fun, but it wasn't going anywhere," says Deitrich, who stayed in Louisville for about eighteen months before moving on. "I thought I would go back to graduate school, become a teacher," he said. Instead, Deitrich returned to Kentucky in 1974, first managing Shelbyville's Science Hill Inn and then creating a restaurant in Bowling Green called the Parakeet.

In the summer of 1977, Deitrich came back to Louisville, opening the first Bristol Bar & Grille on Bardstown Road with his college friend Gossman and Tim Peters. The restaurant, which Deitrich says was modeled on New York City's P.J. Clarke's (called "the Vatican of Saloons" by the *New York Times*), almost immediately became a hit. Deitrich and his partners became local stars. By 1978, the trio had formed a management company and "were feeling…[their] oats," Deitrich says. They opened the Savoy, a downtown restaurant attached to the Natural History and Science Museum, and Langtry's Roadhouse on Shelbyville Road. Though the restaurants were successful, Deitrich was looking for new challenges. "I should have just replicated the Bristol five or six times," Deitrich says, "I would have more money now. But that wouldn't have been as fun."

Instead, after hearing "things weren't wonderful" at his friend Tim Barnes's restaurant, Formally Myra's, Deitrich threw himself into another renovation. "We did some interior work, cleaned it up," he recalls. Deitrich didn't like Barnes's "pretentious" and confusing name for the spot on Grinstead Drive. Because Barnes had sprung for a sign with the word "Ristorante" on it, Deitrich felt the pair "had to leave it"—so the place became Myra's Ristorante and Bar, serving an eclectic menu of dishes, such as trout en papillote, chicken Bel Paese, veal ragout Moroccan and shrimp and black bean sauce. The restoration of Myra's was a success, but the partners "found out after three or four years that we couldn't keep growing enough to support both of us," says Deitrich.

Plus, once again, Deitrich felt the urge to "do something more exciting… to look for a different venue." Around 1987, he began exploring different locations. Then his old partner Tim Peters called, telling Deitrich the old Crescent Theater was available. Bim decided to take a look. Seventeen years after he "had gone to the movies there in 1971," Deitrich began planning a restaurant in the building.

"People thought I was nuts," recalls Deitrich. "Six thousand square feet on Frankfort Avenue? On a street that didn't have a restaurant? Not a single one!" As a bonus, Peters informed Deitrich that the precinct had voted itself dry. "It was because of the Head Rest," Deitrich says. The loud, unruly and sometimes lewd patrons of the musician-friendly

Deitrich's. *Courtesy of Bim Deitrich.*

tavern had so upset residents that they had banned alcohol service in the neighborhood. In the spring of 1988, Deitrich and his partners drew up a petition and began knocking on doors. "We had to promise, 'this place called Deitrich's is not going to be the Head Rest.' I think we won by eight or twelve votes. It turned out that we did a lot more bar business than the Head Rest," laughs Deitrich.

Contractor Mark Campisano and designer Giampaolo Bianconcini restored the 1920s-era tin ceiling and covered the walls of the old theater with French beverage posters from the 1920s and 1930s. The outside of the building featured a *trompe l'oeil* mural of balconies and cornices painted by Jeffery Lee. Inside, beyond the bar, Deitrich and his team turned the former theater into a dramatic dining space. A 1989 *Louisville Magazine* article described how "movie magic" became "cooking magic":

> From the bar terrace...diners look out over three other levels, the last a shiny, semi-exposed kitchen positioned under flat-black ventilating ducts...Shoulder-height, level-separating walls—with one stairway-and-landing system running left of center down to the kitchen and a long service ramp on the far left—make this single space a series of distinct spaces...Amid the chatter from dozens of tables in the goliath theatre, each terrace has its own identity, its own sense of privacy.

The décor wasn't the only thing drawing raves almost as soon as Deitrich's opened. Many of the "American-European" dishes Deitrich developed at Myra's (soft-shell crabs, Southwest wontons, spinach fettucine) were on the menu. The open kitchen built on the site of the former stage also offered selections from a wood-burning grill such as grilled salmon with sake marinade and pork loin with mustard cassis cream—dishes Louisville had never seen before. Reviewers called it a "bright-lights-big-city culinary palace" with "delicious, interesting food served with style." A 1989 article described how "the Old Crescent Theatre's decent-sized [parking] lot has been jammed, seven days a week," noting that "street parkers and curious drivers slowing down on their way to St. Matthews or downtown" added to the throng. Years later, the same reviewer reminisced about Deitrich's, "The food, the dining room were great, but that bar—it was where everybody wanted to be."

The exuberant nature of the rectangular former lobby space was partially the result of excellent remodeling—with an oak bar, a terrace to gaze out over diners and the chance for overflow crowds to spill out through the immense French doors onto the sidewalks of Frankfort Avenue in pleasant weather. But it was also, according to Deitrich, that "prepsters from Indian Hills needed a new home and it was *en masse* in one night" when Susan Seiller closed the former Bauer's. "All of a sudden I look out, and there's fifty people in there," says Deitrich. "They became regulars." Deitrich admits that, at times, "people got tired of walking through the crowd at the bar." But the scene was one of the hottest in Louisville for many years.

Deitrich's almost immediate success made other restaurateurs take notice. Around 1990, Porcini opened just up the street. Other restaurants followed. Deitrich contributed to the avenue's growth as well, opening Allo Spiedo in 1994 and Red Lounge around the end of the twentieth century.

In 1996, Deitrich switched his "American Brasserie" to a "French Brasserie," introducing a twenty-dollar *prix fixe* menu and offering *plats du jour*. Unfortunately, Louisville was Louisville, and Deitrich remembers that "a lot of people didn't get it." Deitrich thought, "Wow, this seemed like a really good idea," but he relented and switched the menu back.

After the turn of the century, Deitrich realized he had to close his namesake restaurant, though he says he "couldn't accept it emotionally." But "the economy, the overhead" convinced him he had to do it. "After 9/11, big restaurants were not going well," Deitrich recalls, "so, it just ended on one crazy night." There was a "huge crowd," with people stretching so far down Frankfort Avenue that his staff reported seeing street vendors setting up beer stands to service the overflow.

Allo Spiedo and Red Lounge continued for several more years, as even more restaurants, bakeries and coffee shops joined the Frankfort Avenue scene. Deitrich opened (and closed) Primo on East Market Street and then worked as a restaurant consultant. He still believes that openings are "the most fun part of the process" and recently considered doing another restaurant, proudly saying, "I did start the restaurant row on Frankfort." Of the former Masonic Temple that later bore his name, Deitrich "won't say it was the greatest restaurant of all time," but he will say, "It was the greatest space that Louisville has ever seen."

Chapter 40
LA PALOMA

*Ruffling Regulars, Regaining Loyalty with
Small Plates*

Wh Susan Seiller thought she saw another opportunity to revive one
of Louisville's historic restaurants. By the late 1980s, Seiller had become
well known for her work at Jack Fry's, cementing its reputation as an iconic
Louisville establishment. Seiller bought the Brownsboro Road restaurant
(but not the property) from the Bauers and then, as she had with Jack Fry's,
closed briefly before opening again under the original name. "We did some
remodeling but reopened with not a lot of changes," Seiller says. "I kept a
couple of Bauer's items on, and I put some Jack Fry's food on." The reaction,
however, was unkind. Seiller admits, "I didn't please the people who were
looking for Jack Fry's, and I pissed off the people who were looking for
Bauer's." After taking stock of the dismal reception, Seiller decided to take
the space in a completely different direction—Mediterranean.

"I had read about the health benefits of the Mediterranean diet," says
Seiller, and a friend had mentioned what Joyce Goldstein was doing with
the food of the region at her San Francisco restaurant, Square One. Seiller
"liked how much flexibility there was in the cuisine and thought the style
would be perfect for *al fresco* dining on the beautiful property," referring
mostly to Bauer's broad, shaded patio. Around 1990, Seiller shut the doors
and hired Chicago architects and artists to realize her vision of a relaxed
Mediterranean restaurant. Columns, terra-cotta tiles, plants and paintings
replaced the well-worn southern style of the original Bauer's. Both Jack

La Paloma. *Courtesy of Susan Seiller.*

Fry's and Bauer's dishes were gone, replaced by pesto minestrone, porcini manicotti and pollo romesco. La Paloma was taking flight.

"The neighborhood really embraced it," Seiller says, "and others liked it too." Local food writers still cherish memories of La Paloma's interior, with one claiming it had "an ambience that had me nearly in a state of Nirvana." Another remembered the restaurant's "classy Mediterranean-influenced food, as well as La Paloma being "the first (and one of the fewest) to offer entrées at two different sizes and prices." Diners were offered "petit" or "grand" sizes of then-novel dishes such as tuna gremolata and fettuccine puttanesca. "That was the first time Louisville had done small plates," Seiller says. "I mean, we had tapas and stuff!" Hummus and vegetables, chicken chermoula, shrimp salpicón and even air-dried bresaola were available, and diners crowded back into the beautiful space.

But as La Paloma grew more popular, Seiller's life grew more hectic. "I was getting married," she recalls. "To have two restaurants and a spouse, it was too much. Something had to go." Seiller told her fiancé, who was also her business partner, that she had to bow out. In 1994, Atlanta's Azalea opened a branch at the site. La Paloma was no more, but Louisville's taste for tapas was ignited, and as of this moment, the city's appetite for small plates has yet to cease.

BIBLIOGRAPHY

Benedict, Jennie C. *The Blue Ribbon Cook Book.* Louisville, KY: John P. Morton & Company, 1904. Reprint, Lexington: University of Kentucky Press, 2008.

Birnbach, Lisa. *The Official Preppy Handbook.* New York: Workman, 1980.

Dick, Erma Biesel. *My Old House.* Louisville, KY: Beechmont Press, 1988.

———. *The Old House Holiday & Party Cookbook.* New York: Cowles Book Company, 1969.

Edge, John T. *Hamburgers and Fries.* New York: Penguin, 2005.

Falk, Gary. *Louisville Remembered.* Charleston, SC: The History Press, 2009.

Flexner, Marion. *Out of Kentucky Kitchens.* New York: American Legacy Press, 1949.

G.A.R. Souvenir Sporting Guide. New York: Wentworth Publishing House, 1895.

Godbey, Marty. *Dining in Historic Kentucky.* Kuttawa, KY: McClanahan Pub. House, 1985.

Hasenour, Marcia. *Hasenour's.* Louisville, KY: Hasenour Press, 2001.

BIBLIOGRAPHY

Hill, Roland L. *I Recommend.* Torrance, CA: DeLaney and Company, 1948.

Hines, Duncan. *Adventures in Good Eating.* Bowling Green, KY: 1947.

Hogan, David Gerard. *Selling 'Em by the Sack.* New York: NYU Press, 1999.

Jakle, John A., and Keith A. Sculle. *Fast Food.* Baltimore, MD: Johns Hopkins University Press, 1999.

Kitchen, Denis, and Michael Schumacher. *Al Capp.* New York: Bloomsbury USA, 2013.

Kleber, John E., ed. *The Encyclopedia of Louisville.* Lexington: University Press of Kentucky, 2000.

K'Meyer, Tracy E. *Civil Rights in the Gateway to the South.* Lexington: University Press of Kentucky, 2009.

La Bree, Ben. *Notable Men of Kentucky at the Beginning of the 20th Century.* Louisville, KY: G.G. Fetter Print Co., 1902.

Liebs, Chester H. *Main Street to Miracle Mile.* Baltimore, MD: JHU Press, 1985.

Louisville Fifty Years Ago… Louisville, KY: C.T. Dearing Print Co., 1923.

Mariani, John F. *Encyclopedia of American Food and Drink.* New York: Bloomsbury USA, 2013.

Miller, Kenneth L. *Stewart's: A Louisville Landmark.* Louisville, KY: Carraro's Art Print & Publishing Co., 1991.

Overy, Ken, ed. *The New York Times Complete World War II, 1939–1945.* New York: Black Dog & Leventhal Publishers, 2013.

Parrish, Thomas. *Restoring Shakertown.* Lexington: University Press of Kentucky, 2005.

Seekamp, Alwin, and Roger Burlingame. *Who's Who in Louisville.* Louisville, KY: Louisville Press Club, 1912.

BIBLIOGRAPHY

Theiss, Nancy Stearns. *Oldham County.* Charleston, SC: The History Press, 2010.

Thompson, Ashlee Clark. *Louisville Diners.* Charleston, SC: The History Press, 2015.

Tifft, Susan, and Alex S. Jones. *The Patriarch.* New York: Summit Books, 1991.

Turchi, Kenneth L. *L.S. Ayres and Company.* Indianapolis: Indiana Historical Society Press, 2012.

Wallis, Frederick A., and Hambleton Tapp. *A Sesqui-Centennial History of Kentucky.* Hopkinsville, KY: Historical Record Association, 1945.

Yater, George H. *Two Hundred Years at the Falls of the Ohio.* Louisville, KY: Heritage Corporation, 1979.

Authors' note: Books of this nature rely heavily on contemporaneous newspaper and magazine articles and Internet-based information. An expanded bibliography and full photo credits are provided at www. lostrestaurantsoflouisville.com.

INDEX

A

Afro-German Tea Room 146,
      147, 148
Aydlett, James 153, 154

B

Ballard, Jenny 109, 110
Barnes, David 144
Barnes, Tim 152, 153, 154, 156
Bauer, Charles F. "Skee," Jr. 16
Bauer, John 15
Bauer's Since 1870 15, 16, 17, 18,
      158, 160, 161
Beam, William 125, 126
Benedict, Jennie C. 31, 32, 33, 34
Benedict's 31, 32, 33, 34
Bingham, Barry, Sr. 25, 26, 27,
      93, 125
Birkla, Estel 62
Blue Boar Cafeterias 60, 61, 62,
      63, 64

C

C-54 Grill 105, 106
Cafe Metro 129, 141, 142, 143,
      144, 145
Canary Cottage 56, 57, 58, 59
Cary, Kathy 134, 135, 136, 137
Casa Grisanti 127, 128, 138, 139
China Inn 53, 54
Chin Jack Lem 53
Chin Ming 53, 54
Chin, Richard 54, 55
Chin, Roosevelt 54, 55
Colonnade Cafeteria 44, 45, 46, 47
Corbett, Dean 140
Crouch, Michael 144
Cunningham, James N. "Cap" 48,
      49, 50
Cunningham's 48, 50, 107
Cunningham's 49
Cuscaden, George V. 19, 20
Cuscaden's 19, 20

INDEX

D

Deitrich, Bim 135, 139, 152, 153, 155, 156, 157, 158, 159
Deitrich's 155, 156, 157, 158, 159
de la Torre, Maggie 150, 151
de la Torre, Miguel 150, 151
De la Torre's 150, 151
Des Ruisseaux, Richard 118
Dick, Erma Biesel 86, 94, 95, 96, 97, 98, 99, 116
Duncan, Harry 51, 52

E

Erpeldinger, Frank 25, 26, 27

F

Ferd Grisanti's 127, 128, 129, 130
Fig Tree 134, 135, 136, 137
Flexner, Marion 14, 21, 23, 24, 27
Foster, Frank 131, 132, 133
French Village 56, 59

G

Gabriele, Vincenzo 138
Garber, Ed 141, 142
Garr, Robin 17, 120, 129, 140, 151
Goheen, Martha 29
Grisanti, Albert 127
Grisanti, Don 138
Grisanti, Ferd 127, 128, 129, 130
Grisanti, Michael 138
Grisanti, Paul 128, 129
Grisanti, Vince 128, 129

H

Hadley, Mary Alice 59, 97
Haner, Greg 21, 22, 23
Hasenour, Ed 73, 74, 75, 76, 77, 78, 111

Hasenour, Lee 77
Hasenour, Marcia 74, 77, 78
Hasenour's 73, 74, 75, 76, 77, 78
Haynes, Greg 46
Heideman, Phyllis 136
Hicks, Daynon and Mary 85, 86, 87
Hick's Drive-in 87, 107, 108
Hines, Duncan 57, 66, 97
Hoe Kow 85, 115, 116, 117, 118, 119, 120

J

Jay's 131, 132, 133
Johnson, A.W.B. 60
Johnson, L. Eugene 60, 63
Johnson, Wes 64
Johnson, Wesley 63

K

Kaelin, Carl 69, 70, 71
Kaelin, Margaret 69, 70
Kaelin's 69, 70, 71, 72
Kattermeier, Ralph 125
Kern, Walter and Leaudra 110, 111
Kolb, Al 13, 14, 21
Kolb's Tavern 13, 14, 21
Kremer, Elizabeth Cromwell 59
Kunz, Fred 42
Kunz, Jacob 38
Kunz, John 42
Kunz's 38, 39, 40, 41, 42, 43
Kupie Lunch 85, 86, 87
Kupie Restaurant and Lounge 87

L

La Paloma 17, 160, 161
Leong, George 116, 117, 118, 119, 120
Leong, Laura 85, 116, 117, 119, 120
Leo's Hideaway 91, 92, 93

Leo's Twinburger 68, 91
Liberty Inn 54, 116
L'il Abner's 112, 113, 114
Little Tavern 51, 52
Luvisi, Ernest 80, 81, 82, 83, 84
Luvisi, Lee 80, 81, 82, 83, 84
Luvisi's 80, 81, 82, 83, 84

M

Mattei, Dorina 127
Mazzoni's 14, 21, 22, 23
Melrose Inn 109, 110, 111
Miller, Hayward "Haywood"
    103, 104
Miller, Rudolph, Mr. and Mrs. 28,
    29, 30
Miller's 28, 29, 30
Montedonico, Tony 13
Mooser, Jenna 144
Myra's 153, 156, 158

N

Neuhauser, Ken 143

O

Old House 28, 86, 94, 95, 96, 97,
    98, 99, 116

P

Pekarsky, Stanley 134, 135, 136
Plantation 88, 89, 90
Pryors 107, 108

R

Raque, Irma 69, 70, 71, 72
recipes
  apple crisp 148
  Chicken Tetrazzini 103
  luncheon rolls 34

rolled oysters 23
  Salisbury steak 64
  Sauerbraten 78
  war sui gai 120
Reigler, Susan 32, 101, 103, 144
Robertson, Father Vernon 147, 148
rolled oysters 14, 21, 22, 23, 154
Runyon, Keith 39, 97, 98, 100,
    101, 103, 113, 114
Rupp, Alan 111

S

Schroeder, Dennis 144
Seiller, Susan 158, 160, 161
Senning, Carl and Minnie 36
Senning's 36, 37
Shepherd, David 141, 142, 143, 144
Shepherd, Nancy 129, 141, 142,
    143, 144, 145
simmons 123, 124, 125, 126
Simmons, Ray 123, 124, 125, 126
Sinnott, Eric 144
Sixth Avenue 138, 139, 140
Smiser, Ann and Jack 109
Southwind 107, 108
Stebbins, George 66, 68
Stebbins Grill 66, 67, 68, 91
Stevens, Mark 140
Stewart Dry Goods 100, 101, 102,
    103, 136
Stewart's Orchid Room 100, 101,
    102, 103
Swizzle 67, 68

T

Timothy's 152, 153, 154

V

Vienna Restaurant 25, 26, 27

W

Weil, Leo 68, 91, 93
Weist, Herman 105, 106
Wheeler, R. Menter 56, 59

Y

Yang, Frank 140

ABOUT THE AUTHORS

Michelle Turner, a practicing attorney, loves restaurants, recipes, photography and cooking. Stephen Hacker enjoys reading, eating and helping Michelle cook. A writer and brand strategist, Stephen has worked for many well-known brands, as well as served as editor of *Eater Louisville* and written for magazines such as *Louisville* and *STORY*. Together, Michelle and Stephen produce an award-winning food blog, Gourmandistan, at www.gourmandistan.com.